CHARIOTS OF THE DAMNED

CHARIOTS OF THE DAMNED

Helicopter Special Operations from Vietnam to Kosovo

**Major Mike McKinney
and Mike Ryan**

THOMAS DUNNE BOOKS
St. Martin's Press ᴹ New York

THOMAS DUNNE BOOKS.
An imprint of St. Martin's Press.

CHARIOTS OF THE DAMNED. Copyright © 2001 by Major Mike McKinney and Mike Ryan. All rights reserved. Printed in the United States of America. No part of this book may be used or reproduced in any manner whatsoever without written permission except in the case of brief quotations embodied in critical articles or reviews. For information, address St. Martin's Press, 175 Fifth Avenue, New York, N.Y. 10010.

www.stmartins.com

ISBN 0-312-29118-3

First published in Great Britain by HarperCollins*Publishers*

First U.S. Edition: July 2002

10 9 8 7 6 5 4 3 2 1

CONTENTS

PREFACE

It is my duty, as a member of the Aerospace Rescue and Recovery Service, to save lives and to aid the injured. I will be prepared at all times to perform my assigned duties quickly and efficiently, placing these duties before personal desires and comforts. These things I do – that others may live. **ARRS Code.**

This book has been written to commemorate the courage and flying skills of the helicopter pilots of the US Armed Forces. From Korea to Kosovo, there have been many outstanding examples of heroic acts performed during rescue attempts and Special Forces operations, while under enemy fire. This book looks at some of these missions in detail, with respect to their background, planning and execution, and how the US Armed Forces will enhance and develop its capabilities in the new Millennium. The sophistication of helicopters has changed dramatically over the last few decades. However the pilot is still at the controls and without his or her flying skills even the best helicopter in the world is useless. These pilots remain an inspiration to us all. Their courage is evident through their willingness to put their lives on the line for others without a second thought.

Today's Special Forces pilots and their Combat Search and Rescue colleagues are among the most respected of military aviators. Their ability to undertake highly dangerous missions, deep behind enemy lines to rescue downed aircrew and support Special Forces teams is greatly admired and appreciated throughout the US Armed Forces, as well as other NATO and UN members.

ACKNOWLEDGEMENTS

In memory of my mother, Mary Ryan and my father, Michael Ryan.

I would like to thank the following people for their help, without it there would have been no book. Sgt Charles 'Chuck' Roberts and Joan Prichard AFSOC, PA USAF, Jennifer Koyama, Department of the Air Force, Washington, DC. Lt Col Kurt Stinemetz, USMC. Ben Abel, PA, 160th SOAR. Department of the U.S. Navy. Pete West, Artist/illustrator for the great computer graphics. David Oliver, for the Scott O'Grady photograph. Popperfoto. Ronald Wong, for the superb combat paintings. All of the following, for their stories and opinions on "Chariots of the Damned": 'CAL'; 'TWO SCOOPS'; 'GUNSLINGER'; 'GINGA'; 'SKEETER'; 'DOCTOR LOVE'; 'BYKER JOE'. Special thanks to AFSOC PA (Air Force Special Operations Command Public Affairs) and SOCOM (Special Operations Command) for all their help.

Special thanks to my co-author, Capt Mike McKinney, for his half of the book. Flying for the 'Special Operations Group' and writing a book at the same time is very hard going. Thanks also to Ian Drury and Rachel Murawa, for believing in the project.

Finally, to my wife Fiona, and my daughters, Isabella and Angelina. Thanks for supporting me during the long months I spent away from home, whilst carrying out the research for this book.

THIS BOOK IS DEDICATED TO THE HELICOPTER PILOTS OF THE UNITED STATES ARMED FORCES, FOR THEIR COURAGE IN PAST, PRESENT AND FUTURE CONFLICTS.

AUTHORS' NOTE

In the interests of American national security, certain mission details have been changed or left out. This is to protect the lives of aircrews operating in potential conflict areas such as the Gulf and Kosovo.

INTRODUCTION

Helicopters have been associated with special operations since their introduction into aviation. Near the end of World War II, the Sikorsky YR-4 was rushed to the 1st Air Commando Group, forefathers of today's Air Force Special Operations Command. On 25 April 1944, the Air Commandos conducted the very first helicopter combat rescue. It took Lt Carter Harman several days to complete the rescue that began with the crash landing of a British L-1. The YR-4 was woefully under-powered, only having a 175-hp engine. In the thin Burmese air, this created quite a precarious position for Harman. Not only was he operating the helicopter at the edge of its envelope, he also had to contend with simply learning to fly this new type of aircraft. Due to maintenance problems the 500-mile journey would take him several days to complete. Exhibiting the determination and ingenuity of the Air Commandos, Harman soldiered on, strapping extra fuel tanks to the helicopter just to make the trip. Harman could only take out one British soldier at a time due to power limitations. After the second soldier was evacuated, the mission was again put on hold by a stubborn engine and thunderstorms. Finally, on 26th April, the last soldier was rescued and Lt Carter Harman had earned a place in aviation history.

The catalyst for the development of special operations helicopters occurred during the Korean War. Helicopters played a major role in moving troops and supplies throughout the conflict. Their true utility quickly became evident to military planners. Special operators once again called upon helicopters to conduct some very unique missions. The newly-formed US Air Force developed a special operations airlift unit under the name, the 581st Air Resupply and Communications Wing (ARCW). The name looked innocent enough yet their mission was to conduct psychological warfare against the forces of North Korea. Much like the Air Commandos of World War II fame, the wing was composed of numerous types of aircraft, each with a different mission. B-29s, C-54s, C-119s, SA-16s, and H-19s all served with the 581st and flew countless missions across enemy lines, most of them at night. For security reasons, the helicopters were collocated with other H-19s of the 2157th Air Rescue Squadron, a fact that did not hold well with the rescue squadron personnel. Operating almost exclusively at night, the H-19s were tasked with delivering covert teams inside North Korea. As a secondary mission, they also participated in several rescues of downed aviators – a common theme for the future. The men of the 581st can truly be considered the first helicopter special operators yet their murky history remains untold.

Historically, Special Operations Forces (SOF) have only been generated in time of war. The need for SOF seems to fade during peacetime. This was also the case during the Vietnam War. Once again, the Air Force was tasked to provide a SOF helicopter force only after the war escalated. In 1965, the 20th Helicopter Squadron (HS) became the first dedicated SOF helicopter unit in the theatre. Initially using Sikorsky CH-3C 'Charlies', the unit became known as the 'Pony Express' because of their callsign. They supported the secret war fought by the now famous Military Assistance Command Vietnam – Studies and Observations Group, or MACV-SOG. MACV-SOG units operated behind enemy lines using teams of Special Forces soldiers and indigenous guerillas. The 20th HS changed to the 20th Special Operations Squadron (SOS) and officially adopted the name 'Green Hornets' after they received the Bell UH-1F/P Huey. The name is in reference to the hovering capability of the helicopters and the sting of their 7.62mm miniguns and rocket pods used for fire support. In 1967 a second squadron was added, the 21st SOS, nicknamed the 'Dust Devils'. The 21st was organized by absorbing the CH-3s of the 20th SOS. They remained at Nakhon Phanom Air Base in northern Thailand while the 20th moved primarily to Nha Trang Air Base in South Vietnam for the remainder of the conflict. The Dust Devil nickname refers to the dust swirl caused by the helicopters' rotor wash. Enemy forces felt that the Devil was responsible for inflicting the pain on them that seemingly emanated from the dust swirl. Each squadron worked directly for MACV-SOG forces. The 20th had responsibility for the southern region, while the 21st operated in the northern region. The 21st traded in their tired CH-3Es for the larger and more powerful CH-53C in 1970. As the war in Vietnam drew to a close, so did the SOS units. The 20th deactivated in 1972 while the 21st stayed active until 1975. Today, both units have been reactivated and their exploits form a major portion of this book.

After the end of the Vietnam War, special operations again took a back seat to other areas of the military. It took the Iranian hostage rescue disaster known as Desert One to finally give vitality to the special operations community. The early 1980s saw the development of Army special operations aviation, first known as Task Force 158 and later Task Force 160. Also money began finally flowing to Air Force special operations units, both helicopters and airplanes. SOF helicopter units have since been used in every major US conflict from Grenada to Serbia. Time and again these units have proven their worth by operating flawlessly despite major obstacles. It is important to point out however, that not all missions have gone as planned and many brave men have lost their lives in both training and live operations. In a small community like SOF these missions and losses have far-reaching effects on how business is conducted. Today, SOF helicopter units stand as some of the most capable and dependable units in the US military. As has been the case on numerous occasions, SOF helicopters have been called upon to deploy and act in whatever capacity at a moment's notice. Direct action raids, combat search and rescue (CSAR), hostage rescues, and snatches are just a few examples where United States' SOF have been called upon. The men and women who fly and maintain these helicopters take great pride in being on the 'tip of the spear' for the United States. They are all volunteers into the community and possess a great deal of loyalty and devotion to the job. In today's military, where a bustling economy has pulled many military members away, SOF units tend to have high retention rates. This despite the fact that at the same time these units also have some of the highest deployment rates.

There would be no purpose for this book if it were not for the existence of special operations ground forces. The sole purpose of special operations helicopters is, in military-speak, to support the customer. That customer might be a Navy SEAL team, a Marine Force Recon team, or a downed aviator. In the end, what matters most is accomplishing the mission. Integral players to nearly every one of these operations are the helicopter crews. They provide the means of transportation, the 'bus drivers' of the SOF community. The term 'special operations' brings with it an air of secrecy and mystery. Special operators are often thought of as knife-wielding war mongers, but this bears little resemblance to the truth. What makes a special operator 'special' is the training and preparation that he must endure in order to be effective. SOF helicopter pilots are no exception. The basic skills taught to nearly every helicopter pilot in the military form the framework for the SOF training. This is evident in the makeup of the various crews mentioned in this book. Each branch of service organizes SOF differently. In the Air Force, SOF helicopters are organized under a separate command, the Air Force Special Operations Command (AFSOC). Using MH-53J/M Pave Lows, they work closely with the remainder of AFSOC, MC-130 and AC-130 aircraft. Although many times considered SOF, USAF Rescue Squadrons flying HH-60Gs are not under AFSOC control yet possess many of the same skills as the SOF units. The Army has a unit similar to AFSOC called the 160th Special Operations Aviation Regiment (SOAR). Operating almost completely separate from the bulk of Army Aviation, the 160th SOAR is equipped with MH-6, AH-6, MH-60, AH-60 and MH-47 helicopters. The 160th SOAR provides the main bulk of SOF helicopters in the US arsenal. The Marines adopt a different approach. Before a Marine Expeditionary Unit (MEU) sails on its rotation at sea, the helicopter crews are trained to conduct special operations missions. Once training is completed the unit is designated Special Operations Capable, or MEU-SOC. The Marines do not specifically single out a unit to have this SOC status, but train all the crews to that standard. Finally, the Navy does not have a traditional SOF helicopter force, but does possess specially trained and equipped Combat Search and Rescue (CSAR) squadrons. Although CSAR is not a primary mission for SOF, these Navy squadrons and the Air Force's CSAR squadrons can be considered SOF-trained.

This book aims to explore the behind-the-scenes details of some of the more famous missions involving SOF helicopters. Concentrating on the 'bus drivers' instead of the 'shooters', it tells the stories from their viewpoint – one that has not been widely addressed. Occasionally, some details of the ground battle are missing, which helps to focus directly on the actions of the helicopter crews. This is not intended to belittle the ground forces but simply avoids retelling stories that already exist in other books and articles. In essence, this book is meant to be a companion to many of the books found in the reference section, aiming to complete the study of a particular conflict. Finally, the rank of each particular participant is shown during the accounts of the mission

CHAPTER 1
VALOUR IN A VERY SMALL PLACE
Mike McKinney

The turbulence caused by the fall of South Vietnam in 1975 spread throughout the region like wildfire. Cambodia and Laos quickly erupted into chaos with people being rounded up like cattle, many of which were never seen again. The violence of these regimes was not unlike that witnessed during the reigns of Hitler and Stalin. Despite this, no nation was willing to risk a continued fight in Southeast Asia to stop the bloodshed. The United States decided that air power diplomacy would be the means to fly the flag in the region, having sent home nearly all of its ground forces several years earlier. Waiting to be called into action at bases in Thailand and on the sea, was a minimal force of fighters, bombers, tankers, helicopters and other support air-craft. The problem was that there were no clear guidelines as to when this firepower would be used. The Ford administration had adopted a purely defensive strategy, waiting until the smoke cleared to begin making long-term plans. One thing was for sure; the US was not about to stand for more prisoners being taken by any country in the area. When Saigon and Phnom Penh fell, huge efforts were made to ensure that every American citizen was evacuated. It was clear that if provoked, the US would use every means available to guard against further embarrassment. On 12 May 1975, the Khmer Rouge government of Cambodia would test that resolve by seizing the US vessel, *SS Mayaguez*, some 60 miles off the southern coast of the country.

The 21st Special Operation Squadron came to Southeast Asia (SEA) in 1968, acquiring CH-3 helicopters from the 20th Special Operations Squadron. The 21st quickly began operations in support of Military Assistance Command-Vietnam, Studies and Observations Group, better known as MACV-SOG. While the 20th SOS covered the southern portion of the region, the 21st would support the north, an area that included the rugged mountains of Laos and Cambodia. In 1970 the squadron became the only Special Operations squadron to fly the new CH-53C, a much larger and more powerful machine than the CH-3. The CH-53 was a cousin of the HH-53, already in service with the 40th Aerospace Rescue and Recovery Squadron (ARRS) in the region, but there were major differences between the two versions. The HH-53 was capable of air refuelling, and while the CH-53 had the fuel plumbing and probes available, the C-130 tanker aircraft did not, so the 21st SOS went without this capability. To compensate for this fuel limitation, the CH-53s carried 650-gallon auxiliary fuel tanks in place of the normal 450-gallon type carried by the HH-53s. This fuel tank was an ad-hoc fix to the problem and had one major flaw; it was very susceptible to ground fire. The 450 tanks were capable of taking up to a .50 calibre round without exploding; the 650 tanks were simply metal cans.

Koh Tang is in every way a very small island. It is located about 35 miles from the shores of Cambodia, and is nearly insignificant on most maps of the region. In May 1975, very little was known of the island or more importantly, the Khmer Rouge forces guarding it. A hastily formed reconnaissance mission flown by a US Army U-21 turboprop plane carrying several members of the Marine assault force identified two small beaches on the northern part of the island. These beaches appeared suitable for a helicopter insertion. In between these beaches was a strip of cleared land, a pathway that the Marines could possibly use to link up and consolidate their forces. It was hoped that only the gunboat crews that captured the *Mayaguez*, a seemingly easy foe, would defend the island. The helicopters would launch from U Tapao AB in southern Thailand in the early morning hours. Flight time for the H-53s was about one hour and thirty minutes one way, a critical fact for the non-air refuellable CH-53 crews. An important tactical fact to note, brought up by Dr. John Guilmartin in his book, *A Very Short War*, is that the two units involved trained for and fought two very different types of warfare. The Knives of the 21st relied upon stealth and concealment to conduct their missions. Close air support was usually available but operated on an 'on-call' basis. These covert tactics were necessary because in order to survive, the SOF teams inserted by the Knives needed to get in without the enemy's knowledge. On the other side, the 40th relied upon brute force to accomplish their mission. They routinely penetrated deep into North Vietnam to rescue downed pilots, and without the close cover of rescue escort (RESCORT) aircraft, the Jollys would be sitting ducks. In essence, the RESCORT aircraft would burn a path to the survivor to ensure the HH-53 could make the trip. As Dr. Guilmartin states, "The two missions called for two different mind-sets: that of the stalker and sniper for special operations, that of the barroom brawler for rescue". This is important when analyzing the tactical plan for the insertion onto Koh Tang. The Knives were comfortable with approaching the island with little fire support from other aircraft while the Jollys would rather have 'bullied' their way in with pre-emptive strikes carried out on Khmer Rouge positions. What level of fire support is the prime question.

During the planning process, the belief was that some if not all of the *Mayaguez* crew was being held on the island. Any strikes conducted may very well kill or injure the crewmembers. Given the small size of the island and the limited intelligence, the risk was too great to attempt pre-assault fire support of any kind. The only fire support would be supplied by the miniguns of the Knives and Jollys. These facts forced the decision to rely on the cover of darkness and surprise to get the helicopters on the beaches.

The men of the 21st SOS and 40th ARRS had just been through what they thought was the last combat action of the war in SEA. In the month of April, each unit participated in Operations 'Eagle Pull' and 'Frequent Wind,' the evacuations of Phnom Penh and Saigon respectively. Although little enemy fire was experienced during these missions, it was the first taste of combat for many of the young helicopter crews. The majority of the men manning these squadrons had been in-country less than a year. With the limited activity of US forces in the region most of the flight time was spent in the local area. Gone were the days of nearly daily combat missions that honed the pilots' skills to a razor sharp edge. Inexperienced helicopter crews, thrown into an ad hoc plan, would fight the ensuing battle at Koh Tang. Only the training received by these crews would eventually save dozens of lives in the midst of chaos. An interesting side note to 'Frequent Wind' is that as the 21st crews flew from around Cambodia enroute to the *USS Midway*, they flew over Koh Tang. Ironically, several crewmembers commented that the island seemed like a nice place for a secluded vacation.

By 13 May, many of the helicopter personnel were getting some much needed rest and relaxation after the busy month of April. When the warning order came down to prepare for deployment to U Tapao Air Force Base, the first problem was rounding up all the crewmembers. U Tapao was located near the southern coast of Thailand and would be the staging base for helicopter operations. The second problem for the squadrons was generating as many helicopters as possible for the tasking. This was not easy, since the H-53 is a notoriously maintenance-intensive helicopter. The Jollys launched for U Tapao first with their two alert helicopters, followed about an hour later with three more HH-53s. The first CH-53s from the Knives took off shortly after the last Jolly.

Tragically, the first disaster occurred within an hour of take-off. *Knife 13*, carrying a crew of five, plus eighteen Air Force security policemen, suffered a catastrophic failure in the main rotor system. One of the six rotor blades departed the aircraft, sending it immediately out of control. The helicopter crashed in desolate terrain only 36 miles east of Nakhon Phanom and burst into flames. A second Knife circled the crash site but the fiercely burning aircraft destroyed any hope. Crewmembers killed in the crash were Capt James Kays, Lt Laurence Froehlich, TSgt George McMullen, SSgt Paul Raber, and Sgt Robert Weldon. Even before the first shots were fired, the battle for Koh Tang had cost 23 American lives. Slowed by this accident, it would not be until very early on the fourteenth before the final helicopter was in position at U Tapao.

Also alerted for the mission were elements of the 4th Marine Division based in the Philippines and the 9th Marine Division based in Okinawa. Given the non-existence of US ground forces in the region, these Marines would provide the only combat units capable of the assault. The Marines immediately rallied their troops and boarded C-141 transport aircraft to rendezvous with the H-53s at U Tapao. By the end of 14 May, the plan called for 1st Battalion/4th Marines to directly assault the *SS Mayaguez*, while 2nd Battalion/9th Marines would assault Koh Tang carried by helicopters of the 21st SOS and 40th ARRS. There was very little planning accomplished by any of the actual participants. The overwhelming sense of urgency did not allow for any critique of the plan or gathering of additional intelligence. Koh Tang would be assaulted at 0542 hours on the morning of the 15th, barely 24 hours after the arrival of the last helicopter. The Knives would lead the mission, with LtCol John Denham, 21st squadron commander in the lead CH-53. U Tapao lies 190 miles from Koh Tang, which meant that the helicopters would have to depart around 0400 hours. This also meant that there would be little time for the helicopters to loiter once inserting the Marines. The exceptions to this were the Jollys that could air refuel and remain available for contingencies. Covering the assault force from the air would be OV-10 Broncos, A-7 Corsairs, and AC-130 gunships yet they could not open fire until the Marines were in established positions on the beach. Additionally, out at sea were the destroyers *USS Henry B. Wilson*, *USS Harold E. Holt* and the carrier *USS Coral Sea*. Each of these ships would play major roles in the battle.

Knife 21, Denham's helicopter, departed U Tapao at 0414 after an unexplained delay caused by upper levels of the chain of command. Aboard *Knife 21* were Lt Karl Poulsen, co-pilot; SSgt Elwood 'Woody' Rumbaugh, flight mechanic; TSgt Robert Boissonnault, the second flight mechanic and 21 Marines. The remainder of the first wave consisted of *Knife 22, 23,* and *31*. *Knife 21* and 22 would land on the west beach while *23* and *31* would simultaneously land on the east beach. Although the two beaches were only 100 yards apart, for the Marines it could have easily been a mile. Following closely behind the first wave were

Knife 32, and *Jolly Green (Jolly) 41, 42,* and *43.* On average, the Jollys carried about seven more Marines than the Knives due to differences in fuel loads. As the first four CH-53s came within sight of Koh Tang, the rising sun was in their faces. The Khmer Rouge soldiers surely must have spotted the helicopters as their silhouettes rose above the horizon. This gave the gunners about 15 miles of forewarning, or 8 minutes – plenty of time to get prepared. The H-53s flew as low as comfortable, 50 to 100 feet above the flat water, trying to hide as best they could. About 3 miles away, the sound of the approaching helicopters rumbled through the trees on Koh Tang. Waiting until the last possible moment, Denham aggressively raised the nose of the CH-53, bringing it to a low hover over the western beach, then turned to place the ramp towards the tree line before landing. Lt Terry Ohlemeier, in *Knife 22,* followed about 500 feet behind Denham. Suddenly, enemy fire erupted from numerous places in the tree line. Khmer Rouge forces fired everything they had: AK-47s, RPG-7s, and mortars. *Knife 21* was mortally wounded instantly as one of her T-64 engines was shredded. Seeing this deluge of fire, Ohlemeier aborted his approach but still suffered major damage. The Marines exited *Knife 21* and headed for cover. Denham pulled his stricken aircraft off the beach, and immediately jettisoned the 650-gallon auxiliary tanks in an effort to lighten the weight. Literally skipping across the water, *Knife 21* headed out to safety, by now also dumping fuel from the main tanks, futilely trying to save the helicopter. *Knife 22* reversed course and flew between *Knife 21* and the beach providing covering fire for the stricken helicopter. *Knife 22's* right gunner was thrown back from his position as a bullet impacted the buckle of his safety belt. Heavily damaged and losing fuel rapidly, Lt Schramm decided the only course of action was to attempt to make it back to Thailand. Denham successfully got *Knife 21* about one mile offshore but could go no further and ditched into the water. As the aircraft settled it rolled over – three of the crewmembers escaped but Lt Poulsen remained trapped, unable to release his safety straps. SSgt Rumbaugh surfaced and noticed the missing co-pilot. Despite his intense fear of water, Rumbaugh went back inside the helicopter to save his co-pilot. Both he and Poulsen surfaced yet Rumbaugh almost immediately sank below the surface, and unable to swim or deploy his life preservers he would become the first casualty of the day.

Nearly simultaneous to the action on Koh Tang, *Jolly Green 11, 12* and *13* were unloading their Marines aboard the USS *Holt* for the assault of the *Mayaguez*. *Knife 23* and *31* were on final approach to the eastern beach when they heard Denham call "Hot LZ!" over the radio. Maj Howard Corson, one of the senior pilots in the squadron, piloted *Knife 31*. Using a side flare manoeuvre, Corson began his approach to the beach. By the time *Knife 31* came within range, Khmer Rouge gunners had sharpened their aim and hammered the big helicopter. In the back of the aircraft, SSgt Jon Harston and Sgt Randy Hoffmaster returned fire with their miniguns. In the front, Lt Richard van de Geer stuck his AR-15 rifle out of the small air vent in the left window and also returned fire. A large explosion completely severed the front portion of the cockpit caused by an RPG-7 rocket propelled grenade. Lt van de Geer was killed immediately in the blast and Maj Corson was stunned. Somehow Corson managed to land the CH-53 in the surf just offshore. SSgt Harston egressed out of the right side cabin door and moved around to the front of the aircraft. He was shocked to see the nose gone with Maj Corson still seated behind the controls. Harston yelled to Corson bringing him back to reality and he immediately unbuckled his safety straps. When Corson looked to his left it was apparent that van de Geer was dead, then the aircraft burst into flames. He stepped over the tail rotor pedals and directly into the salt water. The fire made it impossible to get van de Geer's body out of the aircraft. Harston realized that he had left the helicopter without his AR-15 rifle and decided to go back in to retrieve it, figuring that he would need it on the beach. He had to swim underwater to re-enter the aircraft under the minigun mount bar in the right door. When he emerged, he noticed several disoriented Marines still inside the burning helicopter. The aft section was completely underwater and the Marines were attempting to break out of the side windows to get out. Harston yelled at the Marines to follow him and the group managed to swim out to safety. One look at the battle raging on the beach and the survivors of *Knife 31* began swimming out to sea. Harston found two more Marines swimming around the aircraft and grabbed on to them since they did not have life preservers. The two Marines and Harston swam away with only one inflated bladder on his life preserver. Suddenly, Harston was shot in his flight helmet about two inches above his eyes. Luckily for him he was wearing a ballistic helmet, capable of stopping the bullet. His helmet split into two pieces and fell into the water. Harston was driven down into the water and nearly knocked unconscious. The Marines that he had just rescued were now returning the favour. Eight men died in the wreckage of *Knife 31*. Unfortunately, the helicopter crashed directly in front of a Khmer Rouge gun position that shredded the eighteen survivors. Five more men died trying to make it to the beach. The enemy fire was so intense that the only choice for the remaining survivors was to swim away from the shoreline. One of the swimmers was a Marine forward air controller (FAC) capable of calling in air strikes. He immediately got a survival radio and made contact with the overhead airborne command, control and communications (ABCCC) aircraft. Just before *Knife 23* landed it was also met by intense and accurate enemy fire. Immediately after *Knife 31's* explosion, the entire tail section of *Knife 23* was shot off, and without the tail rotor, the helicopter began a violent spin to the right. Luckily the helicopter was only a few feet off the ground and the pilot; Lt John Schramm was able to set the aircraft down without further incident. The Marines and now the aircrew raced from the helicopter towards cover on the beach. Lt John Lucas, co-pilot of *Knife 23*, also got on his survival radio and started calling for air strikes. ABCCC quickly organized a flight of A-7 Corsairs to provide much-needed covering fire.

The third wave of helicopters was not far behind. *Knife 32* and *Jolly 41* were scheduled to land after *Knife 23* and *31* on the eastern beach. As Lt Mike Lackey, aircraft commander of *Knife 32*, started his approach he witnessed *Knife 31* explode in a huge fireball as the RPG round detonated. The entire aircraft was engulfed with only the rotor head sticking out of the blaze. Having nowhere to land, Lackey aborted his approach and decided to attempt a landing on the western beach. With *Jolly 41* in trail, *Knife 32* found the other side just as hopeless. Seeing that *Knife 21* had ditched, Lackey decided to concentrate on rescuing the survivors before going in to the beach. The helicopter was very heavy with the Marines still aboard. *Knife 32's* crew began dumping fuel to ensure they had hover ability for the pickup. The fuel rained down on the survivors of *Knife 21* as they floated in the water below. Slowly each man was hoisted into the cabin of *Knife 32* – a process that took about twenty minutes. Lackey apologized to the survivors for dumping fuel all over them and then told them they would have to make their second approach to the island. As one can imagine, the survivors of *Knife 21* were not too keen to this prospect. *Knife 32's* Marines were badly needed on the island as the small force fought for their lives. *Jolly 41* was now low on fuel and had to depart to air refuel with a waiting HC-130. As Lackey brought the massive helicopter back into the landing zone on the western beach, the enemy again opened fire. The left minigun jammed at this critical moment, leaving only the right gun capable of providing cover fire. SSgt Nck Morales sprayed the tree line hoping to keep the enemy's heads down but the fire was overwhelming. Lackey skidded the helicopter in sideways, allowing Morales a better opportunity to shoot. They immediately began taking hits, spraying fuel and hydraulic fluid throughout the cabin. TSgt Mike Olsen, the second flight mechanic noticed that a fuel line located just behind the pilot's seat was hit and spewing fuel everywhere. He ripped off his t-shirt, wrapped it around a screwdriver and jammed it in the hole, temporarily stopping the leak. Morales fell back from his gun as he took a round to the chest. He was severely wounded with a collapsed lung and severed artery but still tried to fight on. As the final Marines left the ramp, *Knife 32* lurched off the beach and headed for Thailand with major damage. The hydraulic system took several hits and the aft ramp fell to the full-down position, acting like a huge speed brake on the flight home. Losing fuel rapidly due to holes in every tank, *Knife 32* struggled to make it to safety. An RPG round that miraculously went straight through the helicopter without exploding made two huge holes in the aft cabin. *Knife 32* made it to U Tapao with less than 100 pounds of fuel in each main tank – about three minutes of flight time. The helicopter had 13 holes in the right engine, a hole through the tail rotor drive shaft, and several holes in the main rotor blades, totalling over 300 holes in all.

The battle for Koh Tang was quickly becoming a nightmare for the US forces. In less than one hour, three helicopters had been shot down and two more taken out of the fight. Worse than that, fourteen US personnel lay dead. Enemy forces guarding Koh Tang were much more powerful and prepared than the helicopter crews had been informed. *Knife 22*, heavily damaged during a failed insertion attempt, was now half way back to Thailand but not out of danger. Escorted by *Jolly 11* and *12*, *Knife 22* just barely made it to the coast of Thailand. The fourth wave, consisting of *Jolly 42*, and *43*, was needed desperately to reinforce the forces on the western beach. Led by Lt Philip Pacini in *Jolly 42*, the flight cautiously approached the island. They had overheard the radio traffic and had a pretty clear idea of the firestorm they were going into. Pacini in *42* and Capt Ronald Purser in *43* decided to try simultaneous landings that would get them out of harms way faster. Both aircraft encountered heavy enemy fire and were forced to abort. The flight headed out over the water to regroup. Pacini and Purser knew the importance of their mission and decided to make another run. On their second run, the same reception was found, but this time they forced the issue and delivered their Marines. *Jolly 42* had taken the worst of the fire with 19 holes in the fuselage and damage to the flight controls. Pacini and crew made it back to U Tapao but the helicopter would not fly again during the mission. The situation on the eastern beach now became the focus. *Jolly 13*, flown by Lt Charles Greer and Lt Charles Brown was tasked with attempting a rescue of the *Knife 23* survivors. Having just unloaded Marines aboard the *USS Holt*, *Jolly 13* was completely empty and able to pull out everyone on the beach. In one of the bravest acts of the battle, *Jolly 13* flew straight into the same enemy fire that had just downed two helicopters without any cover fire. Greer planted the HH-53 on the beach right in front of the survivors' position but the enemy fire was too intense for anyone to risk boarding the helicopter. The left side of *Jolly 13* erupted in a fireball as a flare case, used to decoy infrared missiles, caught on fire. Immediately after that, another fire began on the left external fuel tank. It was time for *Jolly 13* to leave before it became the third helicopter downed on the eastern beach. From above, an AC-130 gunship captured the moment with an infrared camera as *Jolly 13* slowly departed the beach, trailing a long line of flames. In the cabin of the helicopter, an alert Pararescueman jettisoned the flare case and most probably saved the aircraft. The fuel tank fire blew itself out as the airspeed increased and *Jolly 13* headed to safety.

While *Jolly 13* was fighting for its life, *Jolly 41* was back from air refuelling, and making a second insertion attempt on the western beach. Flown by Lt Thomas Cooper and Lt David Keith, *Jolly 41* was the only remaining helicopter from the first wave. Their second attempt ended like the first, heavy enemy fire drove Cooper and Keith to abandon the attempt. During this attempt, the helicopter sustained damage to an external fuel tank resulting in a constant leak and limiting loiter time. Because of this, *Jolly 41* was forced back to the tanker for more fuel. By this time in the battle, at about 0900 hours, the AC-130 and A-7s were making almost constant firing passes at the Khmer Rouge positions. These attacks were effective and the Marines gained a little respite from the fire. On *Jolly 41's* fourth attempt, they finally managed to offload the majority of their Marines, and decided to make one more approach to the island. On their fifth and final attempt, *Jolly 41* offloaded the last of their original Marines and more importantly, brought out several wounded Marines. As *Jolly 41* hovered over the beach, a mortar round landed precariously close, causing Cooper to move to another spot. Just after the helicopter moved, another mortar round impacted at their original spot. Cooper and his crew started their first approach to Koh Tang around 0615. They had been driven off each time by tremendous enemy fire. Four hours later they made their last approach, a testament to the courage and perseverance of the helicopter crews. *Jolly 41* returned to U Tapao but the damage inflicted during the battle made it impossible to contribute for the rest of the day.

The first phase of the battle was over. It was meant to be the first and last phase, but now efforts turned to reinforcing the Marines fighting for their lives on the beaches. This first phase had been a costly one. Fifteen US Marines and Airmen were killed and many more injured. Of the original eleven helicopters tasked with the mission, only three remained airworthy. Three had been shot down, and five had sustained major battle damage. As the battle raged at Koh Tang, a small fishing boat pulled up next to the *USS Wilson*. Aboard this boat was the entire crew of the *Mayaguez*. The Marines could now be extracted from Koh Tang, but they needed to stabilize the situation first. 21st SOS maintenance crews managed to get two more CH-53s flyable, making five helicopters available for the mission. At 1145 hours all five helicopters arrived in the vicinity of Koh Tang. *Knife 52*, flown by Lt Robert Rakitis and Lt David Lykens made the first attempt to the eastern beach. Despite the repeated air strikes, *Knife 52* came under heavy fire from the Khmer Rouge gunners. Rakitis aborted his approach and in the process flew straight over the island. He turned the CH-53 toward the Thai coast unable to insert his Marines. *Knife 51* and *Jolly 43* aborted their approaches as well, instead diverting around to the western beach. Each helicopter cycled into the landing zone while the other provided covering fire support. Lt Dick Brims and Lt Dennis Danielson in *Knife 52* inserted their Marines then pressed toward *Knife 51*, which by now was losing fuel rapidly from a punctured external tank. *Knife 51* almost made it back to U Tapao but had to set down about 80 miles away when the fuel ran out. Another helicopter was out of action. On the western beach, *Jollys 11* and *12* made up the second wave of this phase. Each helicopter escaped with no battle damage, showing that the air strikes definitely had taken their toll on enemy forces. At the end of the reinforcement, there were 202 Marines on the western beach and 20 on the eastern beach. Additionally, the crew of *Knife 23* was still on the beach. The group of stranded men on the eastern beach would be the first to be rescued. *Jolly 43* and *11* refuelled and began their approach back to the eastern beach. Again as the massive helicopter came to a hover Khmer Rouge gunners opened fire. *Jolly 43* was riddled by intense gunfire. A 12.7mm round hit a large fuel line in the left side of the cabin causing a massive fuel spray throughout the cabin. The left engine quit shortly thereafter due to fuel starvation. Capt Roland Purser nursed the helicopter away from the island escorted by *Jolly 11*. Purser did not like the idea of flying two hours on one engine. Over the radio he heard that the aircraft carrier *USS Coral Sea* was in the vicinity. Purser elected to fly to the *Coral Sea* instead of U Tapao. After he landed, his crew and members of the *Coral Sea*'s maintenance section devised a way to repair the helicopter. A piece of rubber fuel hose was fixed in place of the damaged metal section and secured with ring clamps. Aside from numerous bullet holes to the fuselage, *Jolly 43* was ready to get back in the game. This was extremely fortunate since every airframe was needed to get the Marines off the island. As luck would have it, another HH-53C from the 40th was brought into commission and pressed into service.

Darkness was nearing by the time the first extraction attempts were mounted. *Jolly 11* left the *Coral Sea* around 1630 hours and pressed on to Koh Tang. Flown by Lt Donald Backlund and Lt Gary Weikel, they would make the first approach, covered by *Knife 51* and *Jolly 12*. Finally, the Marines and Airmen on the eastern beach got their chance to get out of hell. *Jolly 11* landed and the Marines collapsed their perimeter as they made way for the helicopter. Khmer Rouge gunners tried desperately to take out the helicopter. Backlund's gunners, MSgt John Eldridge and SSgt Harry Cash laced the tree line with minigun fire. *Knife 51* joined in the fray with its miniguns. The aft windows of *Knife 51* were punched out and extra crewmembers fired their GAU-5 machine guns out of the holes. As the last Marines were getting aboard *Jolly 11*, Khmer Rouge soldiers rushed the helicopter. They were cut down by minigun and rifle fire just yards from the aircraft. Finally *Jolly 11* departed, wounded but not down, with all personnel from the eastern beach on board. One Marine, a survivor from *Knife 31*, had been seen earlier trapped near the wreckage of *Knife 23*. *Jolly 12* and *Knife 51* moved in to try and locate the Marine. *Jolly 12* hovered over the hulk while *Knife 51* flew gun patterns for protection. The rescue hoist was dropped in hopes of the Marine climbing on, but there was never any sight of him. *Jolly 12* paid the price for this attempt and was severely damaged. Sgt Jesus Dejesus, *Jolly 12's* flight mechanic, was shot in the leg. The pilot, Capt Barry Walls skilfully managed to put the helicopter on the deck of the *Coral Sea* despite hydraulic, main rotor, tail rotor, and fuel tank damage.

The extraction efforts now shifted to the Marines on the western beach. *Knife 51* made the first pass. Brims settled the helicopter down on the rocky beach and loaded 41 Marines on board. He had just enough fuel to make it to the *Coral Sea*. Next came *Jolly 43*, the helicopter that had previously left the island on one engine. To make matters worse, *Jolly 43's* miniguns were not working; the crew had to use their personal weapons for cover fire. Purser quickly landed and pulled out 54 Marines, the highest combat load of the day. *Jolly 44*, flown by Lt Robert Blough and Lt Henry Mason were ready to make their attempt. They were fresh, having just flown from U Tapao. They had made one attempt previously but did not realize that *Jolly 43* was already on the beach. As these three helicopters started this phase, the sun was well below the horizon and it was quite dark. *Jolly 44* extracted 34 Marines and headed for the *USS Holt* instead of the *Coral Sea*. This decision was made because the Holt was much closer and *Jolly 44* could quickly return for more Marines. The only problem with this idea was that the Holt's flight deck was not made for a helicopter as large as an HH-53. To top it off, *Jolly 44's* landing lights were not working. The immense skill displayed by the crew of *Jolly 44* to land the helicopter on the deck cannot be underestimated. Landing on a deck this small is dangerous in the daylight, but at night, with no lighting, it is suicidal. But this day again illustrates the extraordinary valour of the helicopter crews. *Jolly 44's* next approach to Koh Tang would be its last. Enemy fire again found its mark on an HH-53 as *Jolly 44* onloaded 40 Marines. With one engine out, Blough realized that another approach to the Holt was impossible and diverted to the *Coral Sea*. One more pickup needed to be done to clear the island of Marines. *Knife 51* headed towards the beach. Overhead, *Nail 69*, an OV-10 Forward Air Controller (FAC) used his landing light to illuminate the beach for *Knife 51*. The western landing zone was extremely small, made smaller by a high tide, and nearly impossible to see at night. It took Brims four tries to finally get the CH-53 on to the beach. Darkness induced vertigo and spatial disorientation into both him and Danielson and made them abort their first two approaches. On the third attempt, the helicopter literally landed in the water, but not close enough for the Marines to get aboard. The darkness nearly spelled disaster for the Marines. On his fourth attempt, Brims finally got the helicopter near the Marines. TSgt Wayne Fisk, a Jolly pararescueman that volunteered to go with *Knife 51*, asked to go out and search the area. He wanted to make sure no one was left behind. Fisk's courage was legendary. He meticulously searched the beach while under fire from Khmer Rouge gunners. It was 2010 when Fisk finally got back on board *Knife 51* and the helicopter departed.

Knife 51 became the last US aircraft engaged in combat during the war in Southeast Asia. The battle for Koh Tang has since faded into history. It came at a time when most citizens of the United States simply wanted to forget the entire conflict. The event lasted only fourteen hours yet cost the lives of 18 US servicemen. Including the 23 killed before the mission on *Knife 13*, the total climbs to 41. This represents a figure larger than the number of crew on the *Mayaguez*. Luck and plenty of firepower was definitely on the side of the US personnel this day. The outcome of the battle was hanging by a thread from the very beginning. Had the Khmer Rouge forces decided to mount a concentrated attack on the Marines, it is doubtful they could have fought them off. Simply by analyzing the damage, there also should have been two or three more helicopters lying in the surf. This mission was flown by a majority of young and inexperienced pilots but proves the worth of excellent training. Veterans of the war in Vietnam taught these men how to fly the H-53. They were shown that what is important in combat is not always found in the technical manuals. The men of the 21st SOS and 40th ARRS were determined not to abandon the Marines. Taking a helicopter as large as the H-53 and deliberately placing it in the face of the enemy is a monumental display of valour. But, in times like these, men do things they never felt they had the courage to do. In the end, the courage exhibited by the helicopter crews on that day was summarized in a letter by Gen. George Brown, Chairman of the Joint Chiefs of Staff:

"The success of the unique operation to recover the SS Mayaguez and her crew by the combined efforts of the Air Force, Navy and Marine Corps represents an outstanding display of the versatility, dedication and professional competence of all participants. It is not possible to praise too highly the bravery and determination exhibited by all concerned in the assault on Koh Tang island. The overall operation, fraught with unknowns from the outset and extremely difficult to execute under even the best conditions, was conducted by all airmen, sailors and Marines in the highest tradition of our armed forces."

CHAPTER 2
THE PERFECT RAID
Mike McKinney

One special operations raid stands out above all as the best example of flawless planning, preparation and execution: the raid on the Son Tay prisoner of war (POW) camp. By early 1970, North Vietnam was holding several hundred American POWs, most of them pilots, in prisons in and around Hanoi. Intelligence assets indicated that treatment of these prisoners was in a constant decline. The conditions for an American POW included torture, forced labour, and solitary confinement. Coupled with this was the lack of anything even vaguely considered a healthy diet for an adult male. The POW camp near Son Tay was officially identified by US intelligence sources in 1968. Although identified as a possible camp, it wasn't until May 1970 that it was confirmed that US POWs were being held there. Reconnaissance of the camp included flights by SR-71 Blackbirds and Buffalo Hunter unmanned drones. From these flights, an extensive photo collection was compiled of the camp and the surrounding countryside. The camp was unlike other POW camps in the country. Although lying only 23 miles north-west of Hanoi, the area was isolated and desolate. Conditions were very primitive, obviously the camp was not intended to house prisoners for a long period of time. Immediately outside the prison flowed the Song Con River, which made the possibility of flooding always a problem. The North Vietnamese were upgrading the prison, building new facilities for the guards, not the POWs. However, the work did give the POWs a chance to look beyond the walls of the compound and examine possible escape opportunities.

The genesis of the rescue plan came about in June 1970. It became apparent that the POWs inside the camp were sending signals to influence a rescue. Messages were sent using strategically placed dirt piles and drying laundry, something an overhead aircraft would see but not a guard on the ground. The messages indicated that 55 POWs were in the camp and that they were prepared for a rescue attempt. A westward pointing arrow and the number '8' indicated that the POWs wanted a rescue attempt to occur near Mount Ba Vi, a small mountain located 8 miles to the west. It was assumed by intelligence sources that the POWs were sent there several times a week to gather wood for fires and that the opportunity existed to rescue at least some of the group. As this information filtered through military channels it ended up with Army Brig. Gen. Donald Blackburn in the Pentagon. Blackburn was the Special Assistant for Counterinsurgency and Special Activities (SACSA), and worked directly for the Chairman, Joint Chiefs of Staff (JCS). Blackburn assembled a small staff and conducted a preliminary study of possible rescue options at Son Tay. An initial plan called for a clandestine operative to be infiltrated into the region around Mount Ba Vi, gather intelligence on the work parties and signal waiting helicopters when a rescue attempt was possible. While this option seemed to have a high chance for success, Blackburn thought an operation could be conducted to crash through the prison gates and rescue all of the POWs instead of just a few. Although on the surface this option seemed risky, the remoteness of the camp played perfectly into the plan. In late June, after approval from the JCS, Blackburn assembled a feasibility study group of 15 men.

The study group was tasked with assembling a plan in a very short period of time that would give the highest probability of success. The plan that ensued was to launch a helicopter force from Thailand that would fly through the mountains of Laos and North Vietnam and attack the camp under the cover of darkness. Hiding among the mountains was important since North Vietnam had a very dense air defence system, and the signature of a large helicopter force would easily be detected in the open. Also, since Son Tay is located close to the foothills, the element of surprise would be greatly enhanced for the raiders. Surprise was of the utmost importance to ensure that the guards inside the compound would not be alerted to the impending rescue attempt. Another benefit to the raiders was that by 1970 it became clear that the US was not willing to commit any conventional ground forces into attacks within North Vietnam. Although road-watch teams had been infiltrated to recon the Ho Chi Minh trail for many years, most of these were very small and usually operated within Laos or Cambodia. As a result, the North Vietnamese had become complacent about the prospect of a US assault on their homeland. The war to many of those in the North was confined to the sounds of US fighters and bombers. Hopefully, this meant that the guards within the Son Tay prison would not get unduly excited with the sound of aircraft nearby.

The Son Tay raid stands as one of the most daring special operations plans ever devised. A hand-picked group of USAF aircrew and US Army Special Forces raiders would depart from various bases in Thailand, fly in tight formation through the mountains, assault the prison, and return all of the POWs unharmed. The primary assault helicopters would be five Sikorsky HH-53Cs, known as Super Jolly Green Giants. One smaller Sikorsky HH-3E Jolly Green Giant helicopter would be used to crash land directly into the prison compound and provide the shock force for the assault. The helicopters would be refuelled by Lime flight, two HC-130P tankers launching from Udorn AB, Thailand and escorting the helicopters to the North Vietnamese border. For final navigational guidance to the objective, the helicopters relied on two MC-130E Combat Talons from Nakhon Phanom AB, Thailand. These aircraft had very precise navigational equipment as well as terrain following radar enabling the force to accurately weave its way through the mountainous terrain of northern Laos and North Vietnam. The final part of the assault package came from A-1 Skyraiders also launching from Nakhon Phanom. They were to provide the much-needed close air support firepower for the raiders, the only such support in the force.

Brig. Gen. Leroy Manor was selected as the overall commander of the mission. He was in command of the USAF Special Operations forces at Eglin Air Force Base and known as a consummate organizer. It was on his shoulders that the success or failure of the mission would ultimately fall. Since the raid would be conducted at night, weather and illumination conditions had to be perfect. There needed to be cloudless skies for the air refuelling, very little wind and turbulence in the mountains, and one-third to one-quarter moon, 35 degrees above the horizon to provide the necessary visibility. Air Force meteorologists informed the planning group that the best window of opportunity for these perfect conditions was around 21 October. This left less than four months for Gen. Manor and his staff to select and train the rescue force. Immediately it became apparent that the only helicopter forces in the theatre having the capabilities needed to fly the mission were USAF rescue forces. The men of the Aerospace Rescue and Recovery Service (ARRS) were the only helicopter crews that routinely penetrated deep inside North Vietnam to rescue downed airmen. Their training was optimized for this mission and better yet, so too were their helicopters. While there were Air Force Special Operations helicopter units in theatre, none of them were equipped with air refuellable helicopters. Lt Col Warner Britton, a member of the initial planning staff and veteran of several tours in the theatre, became the lead helicopter pilot and began the process of selecting the most capable crews. Britton began recruiting the individuals he thought were the most capable in the ARRS forces. Of the 28 helicopter aircrew that volunteered for the mission, 27 came from ARRS units, the remaining from the 703rd Special Operations Squadron. Additionally, of the 12 pilots, there were two Captains, six Majors, and four Lt Colonels. Clearly, the Son Tay helicopter pilots were some of the most experienced pilots in the Air Force.

One of the pilots selected, Maj Frederic 'Marty' Donohue, was a veteran of over 130 combat missions in the theatre. He was also one of the most experienced pilots in the Sikorsky HH-53 – the aircraft chosen for the mission. In 1967, he actually picked up the very first USAF HH-53B from the Sikorsky plant in Connecticut and flew it down to Eglin AFB in Florida. While the planning staff was feverishly working on the rescue plan, Donohue was preparing for a trans-Pacific flight with the HH-53. This flight lasted over nine days and 8700 miles from Eglin AFB to Saigon, South Vietnam, a feat that had never been accomplished in a helicopter. Another one of the 'recruits' was Lt Col Herbert Zehnder. He too had set a world record in 1967 by flying an HH-3E non-stop from Brooklyn Naval Air Station, New York to the Paris Air Show, a distance of 4157 miles. This flight was done to exhibit the new technology of helicopter air refuelling, done by HC-130P tanker aircraft. Little did he know in 1967 just how important his air refuelling expertise would be to the Son Tay rescue mission.

From 26 August to 8 September, the entire rescue force deployed to Eglin Auxiliary Field No. 3 in the Florida panhandle; today known as Duke Field. Training began immediately and was divided into four phases. Using the crawl, walk, run philosophy, the initial training was meant to simply get all of the assault force proficient with the weapons and tactics needed for the raid. During the first phase the helicopter crews brushed up on formation procedures and became familiar with dissimilar aircraft. The air package was exercised together during day and night formation flights during the second phase with numerous long duration missions. In these early phases, the choice had not yet been made as to what type of helicopter would be used for the initial assault into the compound. Both the HH-3 and a UH-1H Huey were examined to determine which was the best choice. The area inside the compound was a maximum of 85 feet in any direction with 65 to 75 foot trees all around. The HH-3 was 73 feet long with a 62-foot rotor diameter, a tight fit by any measurement. While the UH-1 would fit quite easily, it was not capable of air refuelling, was slower than the rest of the helicopters, and could not carry the minimum number of raiders. So difficult was the task that Lt Col Zehnder and Maj Herbert Kalen, the pilots of the HH-3, made 31 separate attempts over 79 flight hours in an effort to fit the HH-3 in to the prison courtyard, succeeding only on the last attempt. Finally, the decision was made that the HH-3 was expendable, it would be crash-landed inside the compound, hopefully only the rotor blades would be damaged and the raiders would be safe in the cabin. To ensure the safety of the raiders, mattresses were placed on the floor of the HH-3 to cushion the blow. A demolition charge would also be placed in the aircraft, set to explode 20 minutes after the end of the assault, destroying the HH-3 and 'surprising' any North Vietnamese guards left in the compound.

The final phase of training finally put all the pieces together, as the raiders and the helicopter crews practised every contingency. With only two weeks left until the first launch window, one final piece to the puzzle remained – the elimination of two guard towers on the wall surrounding the prison. The raiders could not place enough rounds on target in the initial assault to ensure that the guards in the towers wouldn't jeopardize the mission. The only option was to use the firepower of the HH-53s. Maj Donohue and Capt Thomas Waldron were chosen to act as a gunship and fly between the towers while their crew in the back, SSgt Aron Hodges, SSgt James Rogers, and SSgt Angus Sowell engaged the towers with their 7.62mm miniguns. With firing speeds up to 4000 rounds per minute, the three miniguns would shred the guard towers in seconds. This was a very risky manoeuvre because of the proximity to the POW's quarters. There could be no margin for error as the chance of injuring the POWs was just too great. As the crews prepared for the date of 21 October, a final political delay pushed the raid back to the next window beginning on 20 November. While this gave them 30 days more to rehearse, it also meant 30 more days for security to be blown. Even after all of this intense preparation, very few people in the force knew of the exact target. Because of the numerous hours of overwater flight, many of the helicopter crews were convinced they were going to launch an attack on Cuba. In the end, the assault force conducted 170 rehearsals of the mission, totalling over 280 sorties and 790 flight hours. They were honed to a razor sharp edge and ready for action.

On 14 November, the assault force boarded four C-141 Starlifter transports and began the trek to Takhli AB, Thailand. Several months prior, the plan was put in motion to ensure that the HH-53 and HH-3 helicopters were 'stood-down' from Thailand-based rescue units a couple of days prior to the mission and made mission-ready. Upon arriving at Takhli the crews were kept in isolation from the rest of the base and made any last minute preparations. Very little remained that had not already been rehearsed. As luck would have it, a typhoon was threatening the Carrier Battle Group in the Pacific Ocean. This was important because aircraft from this Group would provide diversionary raids to the east of Son Tay in an effort to get the North Vietnamese radar systems to look away from the assault force. Gen. Manor was told that his best chance was on the night of 20 November – a day earlier than he wanted, but definitely possible. The final cut was made on the raiding force, 56 men in total. Intelligence reports stated that they would find approximately 70-80 ill-nourished, weak, and sick POWs. One final briefing was conducted on the evening of the 20 November and the helicopter crews and raiders boarded the C-130s for the short flight to Udorn AB, in the northern part of Thailand. There they transferred to the helicopters, five HH-53Cs and one HH-3E. The callsign of each part of the air package was a different fruit. The A-1s were *Peach* flight, the MC-130s *Cherry* flight, the HC-130s *Lime* flight, the HH-3 was *Banana 1*, and the HH-53s were *Apple* flight. Leading the helicopter formation was *Apple 1*, aircraft number 68-10357 flown by Lt Col Britton, Maj Alfred Montrem, MSgt Harold Harvey, MSgt Maurice Tasker, and SSgt Joh Hoberg. On board they carried 20 raiders, including the ground force commander, Col Arthur 'Bull' Simons. *Apple 2*, aircraft number 68-10361, was flown by Lt Col John

Allison, Maj Jay Strayer, TSgt William Lester, TSgt Charlie Montgomery, and SSgt Randy McComb. They carried the remainder of the support group, 22 raiders and acted as *Apple 2's* wingman. *Apple 1* and *2* would land just outside the southern wall of the prison, deposit their force, then fly to a laager site a few miles away and await the exfiltration call. The first aircraft over the prison would actually be the third in the formation, *Apple 3*, aircraft 68-8286. The crew and mission of *Apple 3* did not change from the training phase, about 3 miles from the prison, they would accelerate ahead of *Apple 1* and *2*, come to a near hover just above the cell blocks and provide the initial fire support. The final two HH-53s, *Apple 4* and *5*, were 'slick' aircraft, carrying no raiders. Their purpose was to land on a small island in Finger Lake just miles from the prison and await the call to go in and pull out the POWs. *Apple 4*, 68-8285, was flown by Lt Col Royal Brown, Maj Roy Dreibelis, TSgt Lawrence Wellington, SSgt Wayne Fisk, and SSgt Donald Labarre. *Apple 5*, 68-10359, had a crew of Maj Kenneth Murphy, Capt William McGeorge, TSgt David McLeod, SSgt John Eldridge, and SSgt Daniel Galde. Finally, Lt Col Zehnder, Maj Kalen, and TSgt Leroy Wright flew *Banana 1*, HH-3E number 65-12785. They carried the initial assault force of 14 men. These men would be the first to release the POWs and as can be imagined, their sense of purpose was extremely high.

At 2318 hours Udorn time, *Apple 1* lifted off the ground. Seven minutes later the final HH-53 was airborne and the mission began. This was possibly the most critical phase of the mission. Despite the thousands of hours of preparation, the maintenance status of the helicopters was completely out of the hands of the Son Tay planners or crews. The aircraft had to perform flawlessly, for an abort by any of the helicopters could mean the end of the mission. In the cockpits, the pilots turned to the daunting task that lay ahead. While the tension was still there, the months of training, and years of experience began to settle each man down. The flight formed up with *Lime 1*, an HC-130 tanker in the lead, three HH-53s off the right wingtip, and the HH-3 and the remaining two HH-53s off the left wingtip. The HH-3 had to remain closely tucked in behind the HC-130 in order to maintain speed. Using a technique similar to a racing driver, Lt Col Britton and Maj Kalen would 'draft' off of the HC-130 all the way to North Vietnam. The crews had a three-hour flight ahead of them through rugged mountains and penetrating one of the most dense air defence networks in the world. In the back of the helicopters, the raiders could only try to relax and get some sleep. For the first two hours the flight proceeded nearly due north into northern Laos at 1500 feet above the ground. The helicopters would move down and refuel as necessary to ensure enough fuel was onboard to either return to Udorn or continue the mission should an emergency occur. At about 0115 hours, the flight turned to the northeast, the helicopters refuelled one final time and rendezvoused with *Cherry 1*, the MC-130 Combat Talon that would lead them to Son Tay. Due to the speed differences between the aircraft, the C-130s were required to fly at near stall speed, while the HH-3 was flying as fast as was physically possible. Behind them was a second flight comprised of another MC-130, *Cherry 2*, who was leading *Peach* flight, the five A-1 Skyraiders. Precise navigation was critical as each flight wove its way through the mountains and valleys of Laos at low altitude and in total radio silence.

As the flight emerged from the foothills in North Vietnam, the lights of Hanoi could be seen glowing in the distance. This was the time when the mission was most vulnerable. The planners had gone to considerable lengths to analyze the North

Vietnamese early warning radar coverage and to choose the best route. The diversionary air strikes would commence at any moment, turning the radar systems to the east and away from the formations. These strikes so confused and overwhelmed the North Vietnamese system that many of the operators simply quit trying to fight back. At the initial point (IP), a designated final checkpoint 3.5 miles prior to the objective, *Cherry 1* relayed: "zero-seven-two, zero-seven-two hack", the final inbound heading to the helicopters, then accelerated and climbed to 1500 feet to drop flares over the compound. *Apple 4* and *5* broke away from the formation to land at their laager site on an island in Finger Lake, and await the call to pick up the POWs. At the same time, *Apple 3* accelerated to 95 knots indicated airspeed and headed toward the compound for the firing pass, with *Banana 1* close behind. At treetop level, in the darkness, a glaring error was about to be made. The formation was headed toward the wrong objective, a compound only 400 yards to the south that closely resembled Son Tay. Donohue and Waldron noticed the mistake at the very last second and turned to the north. Zehnder and Kalen saw the turn of *Apple 3* and followed, realizing the error. *Apple 3* slowed to a near hover as they reached the outer walls. As the flares dropped by *Cherry 1* illuminated, Sgts. Rogers, and Sowell identified their targets and immediately opened fire.

From their cockpit in *Banana 1*, Zehnder and Kalen had the best view of the opening moments of the raid. The eerie bright white light of the flares lit up the entire compound, then the orange tracers streamed from *Apple 3*, directly on target. The guard towers erupted in a fireball as if they had exploded. *Banana 1* was now seconds from touchdown. Kalen brought the HH-3 in from the west, just above the Song Con River and the compound wall. Sgt Wright in the right door opened fire on the guard barracks located to the south. About 60 feet in the air, the rotor blades contacted trees that had grown taller since the initial plan. The aircraft shuddered violently as the blades sawed through the trees. Kalen nearly lost complete control but kept the HH-3 upright and landed very hard but in the perfect location. Zehnder and Kalen shut the HH-3 down just feet from the prison cellblocks. The raiders in the back felt a hard jolt, but all were safe and immediately began exiting the aircraft. The landing was so violent that a fire extinguisher broke loose from its mount and slammed into Sgt Wright's ankle, breaking it. Meanwhile, *Apple 1* and *2* were still in formation together, and heading for the wrong compound. Allison and Strayer in *Apple 2* noticed the error but elected not to break radio silence. As *Apple 1* landed at the other compound, *Apple 2* turned hard to the north and began their approach as their pararescueman lit up the nearby guard barracks as well with his minigun. Britton and Montrem took off immediately after dropping off their raiders and headed for the holding area, still unaware of the mistake. *Apple 2* called out to *Apple 1*: "Hey you set 'em down in the wrong place buddy, did you let 'em out?!" Simultaneously, Britton noticed the mistake and racked the big HH-53 around to pick up his raiders. A huge firefight ensued at the wrong compound, it turned out to be a military barracks of some nature, and the raiders killed numerous enemy soldiers without any injuries to themselves. Britton landed a second time, then flew the short distance to Son Tay, deposited the raiders in the correct landing zone and left again for the holding area.

The *Apple* flight crews landed in nearby fields, turned up the volume on their radios and anxiously waited for the extraction call. They knew that if the raid went past 30 minutes, something dreadful had gone wrong. SA-2 surface-to-air missiles (SAM) launched at the fighters from very nearby sites, were lighting up the night sky. Meanwhile, the crew of *Banana 1* simply tried to keep from getting killed as a huge firefight erupted around them. The raiders methodically went about their plan, finding many enemy soldiers along the way, but no prisoners. Over the command radio net came: "Wildroot, this is Blueboy, negative items so far, will give a report shortly". This was the first sign that things weren't going as hoped. Blueboy element was the main assault force, delivered by *Banana 1*, and the primary search element. A few minutes later, Blueboy called back and confirmed the worst fears, there were no POWs in the compound. Britton and Montrem received the call, ". . . there's negative items, come in on a normal LZ" and immediately took off enroute to the compound. The extraction went as smoothly as they had practised, with the exception of no POWs. *Apple* flight formed up and headed back westerly, with a huge air battle still in progress. SAMs streaked through the sky trying desperately to find their targets. *Firebird 5*, an F-105G Wild Weasel aircraft was hit and the crew forced to eject over Laos. *Apple 3* remained at the holding area, they were to be the 'clean-up' aircraft in case anyone was left behind. The waiting became tense as they were finally told that all of the raiders were accounted for and they could get out of the country. Enroute, *Apple 4* and *5* were diverted to locate and recover the F-105 crew, a small victory in the entire raid.

During the flight home, everyone relived the moments in their minds; they were completely demoralized. It seemed that the intelligence folks had really screwed up this time. The planners were sure that there had been POWs there, or had it been a clever trap laid by the North Vietnamese? The truth is that

POWs had been at Son Tay, but for reasons still unknown, were moved in July to another camp just a few miles away. In fact, the POWs actually watched the raid unfold, awakened by the decoy firefight simulators and the SAM launches. The most probable reason for their movement was that the CIA, unknown to the raid planners, had begun a program to seed rain clouds over North Vietnam in an effort to flood the rice crops. This was hoped to reduce the amount of food heading to North Vietnamese troops. As the rains fell, the Song Con River rose to a level that threatened the Son Tay prison and the POWs were moved.

While on the surface, the Son Tay raid seems like a complete failure, it did have some unseen effects. The North Vietnamese feared another raid and congregated all of the POWs into two camps in Hanoi. This allowed the POWs to communicate among one another, increasing morale. As the story of the raid circulated among the POWs, told by those who had witnessed it, they realized that their country had not forgotten them. Finally, the North Vietnamese began taking better care of the POWs, again fearing reprisals from the United States. What the Son Tay raiders had done was truly remarkable. They planned, rehearsed, and executed a daring special operations mission, deep in the heart of enemy territory. Their goal was the noblest of all, to rescue fellow countrymen held against their will. The lessons of the Son Tay raid are still echoed today in special operations training; that a mission properly planned and practised can succeed even under the most demanding conditions.

CHAPTER 3
DISASTER AT DESERT ONE
Mike Ryan

The Vietnam War left America feeling battered and bruised. In the case of the US armed forces a feeling of humiliation remained for many years after the fall of Saigon. Sights onboard US aircraft carriers during Operation Frequent Wind, such as American helicopters being tossed overboard into the sea to make space for others to land, were unforgettable. These leaving a bitter taste in the mouths of men who had fought hard for their country in a war that seemed impossible to win, both in military and political terms.

The feelings were that the US armed forces had won the battles, but the politicians had cost them the war. They vowed that this would never happen again, and the military forces of the USA who were down, but far from out, looked for an opportunity to restore their military pride. Next time the outcome was going to be different, or so they thought.

Barely four years had passed since the end of the Vietnam War, when a crisis developed in Iran that was to have a devastating outcome. On Sunday 4 November 1979, the American embassy in Tehran came under attack by supporters of the Ayatollah Khomeini. Sixty six Americans were taken hostage in a bid to force the USA to hand over the pro-Western deposed Shah of Iran. Khomeini and his supporters began to make veiled threats to the United States, that they would hold trials for the American hostages for the alleged crime of spying. They stated that if found guilty they would be executed.

This put intense pressure on American President Jimmy Carter, who had never in his career had to deal with any situation like this. The American public watched in horror, as images on television showed their flags being burned, along with effigies of President Carter. This was too much to bear, as these people seemed to be rubbing America's nose in the dirt. Steadily the demands grew for action to be taken, be it political, or if necessary military. As a gesture, thirteen black and female hostages were released, the remaining white males were to be held and used as political pawns.

The military Hawks in America were itching for a showdown with Iran, however the rules of international diplomacy, demanded that at least some political effort be made to resolve the crisis. President Carter called on the help of the United Nations, and asked for economic sanctions to be imposed on Iran to bring them to surrender, however this failed. Further attempts to use Iranian moderates also came to nothing, and a cold reality dawned on America that the use of force was now becoming ever more likely.

The United States had granted asylum to the deposed Shah, whose regime it had vigorously supported, so there could be no question of handing him over to the fanatical fundamentalist Islamic government that had taken power. Dealing with these people was proving impossible, and the military options clearly had to be examined. In public, President Carter was keen to down-play the military side of his options, however behind the scenes he had formed a special joint task force to investigate the possibilities of exercising his 'Military Option' and how they would extricate the hostages.

President Carter's caution was understandable. The US

Military was keen to go, however there was little enthusiasm from the American public for another war. Carter faced enormous problems in considering a military response. He clearly had a duty to get the hostages back, and knew that a full-scale war with Iran, however successful, was unlikely to effect a rescue. The other problem he faced was that the hostages may be executed as an act of revenge, and the death of just one, would bring about political suicide for him.

The only other viable option, would be a precision attack on the Embassy by US Special Forces. This option was to be known as Operation 'Ricebowl', and a detailed rescue plan was to be formulated with the actual mission name of Operation 'Eagle Claw'.

The plan was incredibly ambitious, there were to be no Iranian casualties, and the hostages were to be spirited away before the Iranians could mount an effective reaction. The US Top Brass knew that such a mission would be extremely difficult, if not impossible for America's Special Forces, who had not performed as well as expected in Vietnam, and had never attempted a mission as complex as this. The only two countries in the world that had a significant Special Forces capability were Britain and Israel and even they doubted if such a mission was realistic and achievable.

Whatever the concerns were, and there were many, America had to get back its Citizens. The joint task force would have to look at many concepts of operations (CONOPS) and analyze each one on its individual merits. The ideas put forward varied greatly in viability. The main problem the United States had was the lack of intelligence on the ground. It would seem incredible today that at this time that the CIA had nobody in Iran and even the layout of the Embassy posed a problem. The mission planners were anxious to get on with their jobs, however with the lack of suitable information, only so much could be done.

The situation was looking bleak, the United States, the world's greatest superpower, openly admitted that they knew little or nothing about Iran. There was no knowledge of airfields, troop positions, local geography or even the most basic information as to where in the Embassy the hostages were held. If there was any comfort to be had in all of this chaos, it was the fact that America had only just formed a new Special Forces unit prior to the hostage crisis. This unit, known as 'Delta Force' was commanded by a highly motivated and determined – Colonel Charles Beckwith.

Beckwith had formed Delta Force after serving with the British SAS (Special Air Service) during an exchange programme. He admired the British Special Forces, so much so that he felt America should have an equivalent unit as soon as possible. The US unit borrowed ideas, training and operational methods from the British which were all but slightly adapted for US operational doctrine. Colonel Beckwith was extremely proud of his unit and was very keen to show the world its capabilities.

This was to be a combined service operation, and as usual there were inter-service rivalries that got in the way of operational sense, with many of the units not having worked together since Vietnam. However, Delta had a trump card. When they attended the joint task force meetings, they always made sure that they were well represented, as a result their ideas were more accepted and understood then those of their other service colleagues. This was imperative, as they fully understood the complexity of the operation and that they would be the key players.

While the hostages remained in the Embassy, there was time to plan a detailed operation, and look at all the rescue ideas in detail. Suggestions were put forward for using parachutes, fixed-wing aircraft, helicopters, trucks, buses and even cars, however the preferred method was to be the helicopter. An emergency assault plan was also hastily put together, in the event that the Iranians started to execute any of the hostages. In this case Delta would fly into Iran at low-level, and on approach to Teheran the aircraft would climb to a suitable height, just east of the city. The Delta Force would then parachute in, and commandeer any suitable vehicles for the journey to the Embassy. They would then assault the Embassy compound and free the hostages. During the next phase they were to fight their way through the city towards Mehrabad International Airport, where upon arrival, they were to set up a defensive perimeter, and await the arrival of transport aircraft. In the event that this option could not be exercised, they were to escape and evade the enemy by moving into the nearby desert. They were then to make their way northwards to Turkey, as it was technically neutral.

The chances of this operation succeeding were virtually zero, and Delta was desperate to formulate a more realistic plan. As the days went by more and more intelligence started to filter through, and the options were narrowed down to just one, which pointed to the plan becoming a helicopter-based operation. Helicopters were used extensively in Vietnam where they continually proved their worth and, although they possessed certain negative points, they were thought to be the best tool for the job.

However the question was raised as to the type of helicopter that should be used. This mission would require a platform that had both good range and load carrying capability. There were several options, CH-47 Chinooks or CH-46 Sea Knights, HH-53s or RH-53s. In the end a decision was taken to use the

53 series as it met most of the operational criteria. The particular model they chose was the Navy RH-53D, known as the Sea Stallion, this had both a foldable tail boom and rotor blades, which permitted them to be carried on aircraft carriers. These helicopters were normally deployed for mine-sweeping missions, so their presence on board a carrier would not cause any undue interest, this was of paramount importance, as the US did not want to compromise mission security.

The RH-53D was the largest helicopter in the US inventory, with full fuel load it could carry thirty people, with a low fuel loading it could carry as many as fifty people. There was no question that the helicopter plan now on offer was vastly superior to the original Delta contingency option worked out in the first days of the crisis. However there was a key critical problem that had to be addressed – fuel. The Sea Stallion had an impressive long-range capability, but it would not be able to fly from the Gulf of Oman to Teheran without refuelling, as the distance to be travelled was about 900 miles. How, when and where would they refuel? These were important questions that had to be answered to enable the operation to go ahead. There were many options put forward. One idea was that Delta would attack and seize an airfield, however this would increase the chances of the operation being compromised, and to kill people unnecessarily would have caused political problems elsewhere in the region. The fuel question was proving difficult to answer, and this was seen by many as being the achilles heel of what was basically a very good plan.

During this time Delta had overcome one other major problem, that being the lack of detailed intelligence on the Embassy, hostage takers and the surrounding areas of Teheran. They now at least had something to work with to plan the delicate hostage extraction problem. They had gone from one extreme to the other, in the early days they new little or nothing about Iran, now the CIA was beginning to give them information overload.

Boxes of information started to arrive at Delta's HQ on a daily basis. Their Intelligence Officer, Wade Ishimoto, struggled to keep on top of it, he knew that every photo and document had to be assessed and analyzed for its importance, and on many nights he was lucky to get four hours sleep. The pieces of the intelligence puzzle soon started to come together, and gradually a framework for the operational planning phase was created. Everybody involved in the operation could see that this was a highly complex mission, and it was evident that each service still had much to do to ensure the gaps were filled in both equipment and personnel.

The only comparable operation that America had performed previously using helicopters for a hostage rescue, was the Son Tay raid in Vietnam. This had been performed by the USAF and compared to the mission that they were about to undertake, it was relatively simple. Although the Son Tay raid failed to accomplish its principle objective of rescuing American prisoners-of-war, it did prove that a well-planned operation could succeed, and was something of a trail blazer for the US Special Operations Group.

Using the intelligence now gained, the operators constructed a detailed model of the Embassy to determine where the hostages were being held, how the rooms were laid out, and even details such as which way the doors opened. They also constructed a mock-up of the Embassy in Yuma Army Airfield in Southern Arizona, to rehearse the mission and evaluate extraction tactics.

The original plan was to bring the helicopters in as close to the Embassy as possible to speed up the rescue, as time was critical in this mission. This however could not be done, due to the fact that the Iranians had anticipated such an attack and had erected wooden poles all around the compound to prevent helicopter landings. This development was brought to light by US Intelligence photos taken from both Satellites and SR-71 Blackbird aircraft operating over Iran. During the operational rehearsals at Yuma one potential resolution to the fuel problem was attempted. Huge rubber fuel bladders would be parachuted into the desert at the RV point with the helicopters, this would dispense with the need for dedicated USAF refuelling aircraft which it was felt were too heavy for landings in the desert. The fuel bladders were massive, each one could hold 500 gallons of aviation fuel, and they were equipped with their own pumps and hoses. There was a downside however – they were very slow in transferring fuel and if they landed in the wrong place, such as amongst rocks, they could not be moved. Each one required at least ten men to roll it, and during an operation like this, manpower levels would be critical.

The big fear was that during the parachute drop a blower, or fuel blivet as they were often called, might hit a parked helicopter and destroy it. This was of great concern, so it was agreed that some trials would take place. The trials were to be carried out at night with real RH-53Ds on the ground. The drop was to be made by C-130s, and it was planned that twelve blivets would be air-dropped. General Gast who was observing the trials with Colonel Beckwith, felt very uncomfortable with the course that the pilots were flying and ordered a change. Amazingly his instincts were correct, ten out of twelve parachutes failed to open due to bad rigging, and the giant blivets hit the ground with great force, exploding on impact like ripe pumpkins. This was a dreadfully embarrassing incident, had it not been for General Gast's revised order, most of the helicopters on the ground would have been destroyed. Subsequent air-drop trials took place which were successful, but there was clearly a significant confidence issue in this method of fuel supply.

As the weeks went by, the parachute riggers worked out a new dropping technique which worked on every practice, with no blivets lost. During a rehearsal at Fort Bragg's Holland DZ, an observer who was an air operations manager for the CIA in Laos, suggested to Colonel Beckwith that he drop the blivet idea as it was far too risky. He pointed out that during the real operation there would be a danger of high winds blowing the blivets off-course with disastrous consequences for those on the ground. This operator clearly knew his business and recommended that they use a dedicated fuel carrying aircraft such as the EC-130. He had been able to land aircraft in places that were thought impossible and was convinced that photos he had seen of possible landing sites could support the weight of an EC-130.

The Air Force operational planners had always dismissed the idea of a fuel-laden aircraft landing in the desert, as they believed that the crust of the desert floor would not support the aircraft's weight (extra fuel tanks contained over 3000 gallons of fuel). This seemed like a fair and reasonable objection, as the Air Force staff planners did not know the exact landing site. There could only be one answer. Put people on the ground. It made perfect sense; if suitably qualified people could land on a site and carry out a detailed survey, including the taking of soil samples, then this objection could be overcome.

Colonel Beckwith was impressed with the idea, as this operator's idea seemed a better bet than the blivet option. He put in a formal request for a reconnaissance mission to be allowed, as this would either confirm or eliminate the EC-130 option. A recommendation was also made to include an Air Force Officer on the mission, as his findings would be more credible to his own service. Carrying out such a mission brought its own risks, such as the possibility of being observed by the Iranians. This would indicate that the Americans were up to something and put them on full alert, making a rescue attempt impossible. Yet it had to continue.

Air-based Intelligence had now identified a possible site for the RV. It was situated in the vast Dasht-e-Kavir Salt Desert, 265 nautical miles south-east of Teheran. The nearest habitation was over 90 miles away, it seemed perfect for the job and subject to the survey this was to be the place. The site was to be known as DESERT ONE.

Although there were still issues and concerns that needed attention, feelings within the planning office were optimistic, everything seemed to be coming together and confidence in Operation 'RiceBowl' was steadily growing. However one of the main issues was concerning the choice of helicopter pilots that had been selected to fly the mission. From day one of the crisis it had been decided and agreed that this would be a combined services operation. Understandably everyone wanted to play their part in the mission to rescue their fellow countrymen who were being held hostage. The choice of using Navy pilots for this operation had been questioned from the start, as it was felt that Air Force pilots would be more suitable for such a demanding long-range, low-level flight. In addition to the Army they had more experience with this type of flying and a different type of flying skill was needed that the Navy pilots simply did not have.

The professionalism of the Navy pilots was never doubted, it was just that they did not seem correctly suited for the job. The

Air Force lost out on this argument and were instructed to leave everything as it was. The Navy had argued that the helicopters to be used in this operation were theirs, and so it would be sensible that they should fly their own machines. A compromise was struck; the Navy would undertake intensive low-level flight training with Delta Force to bring their flying skills up to the standards needed. This solution was accepted and the Navy pilots went into training in Arizona. The learning curve for the Navy pilots was highly demanding – some saw it as a challenge, while others clearly struggled to cope with the changes.

Colonel Beckwith was dubious of the Navy pilots' role in this operation, and felt that it should have been the Air Force pilots that were chosen to fly, after all it was them who had performed the Son Tay raid in Vietnam. Beckwith observed the Navy pilots in training, and felt that they were not coming up to standard and time was fast running out.

In total the Navy had seven crews undergoing training. Although the pilots were precise and careful, they were used to flying in minesweeping operations that required flying in set patterns over an area, looking for anything that would betray the presence of a mine. This called on the pilot to be patient and diligent and although these were impressive skills they were not really what was required for a rescue mission.

The type of pilot that Delta needed on this mission was a daredevil, similar to the pilots that toured America and Europe after the end of World War One – entertaining the people on the ground with their flying skills. The pilot would need to be a quick thinker, someone who could improvise when things didn't always go as planned; flying over Iranian airspace was going to be demanding and nobody would be able to predict every possible danger ahead. Delta was becoming very concerned with the performance of the Navy pilots, they were unable to fly in tight formations at low-level, which was the key requirement. They also found it difficult to fly in 'Flight Regime' – where pilots are required to fly in tight formation, navigating without landmarks and landing in total darkness.

It was felt that one or two of the crews may come up to standard given more time, however the rest just could not make the transition. One pilot even refused to fly because he was scared of flying into combat and was so overcome by his fear that he quit. It was therefore ordered that he be Court-Martialed and restricted to a secure area where he could not discuss the mission. Things also came to a head with the other pilots and they were finally returned to their original units after being sworn to secrecy. Only one was retained for the operation.

General Vaught took up the problem of pilots with General Jones, who reported to the JCS. The J-3 in the JCS at this time was a Marine Lieutenant General named Phillip Shutler. His response was to send a Marine unit of pilots from Air-Stations from both Jacksonville, Florida and another on the West Coast. Due to the problems that had already taken place, many questioned the wisdom of such a decision. It was felt that USAF aircrews should have been provided, but at this time the Marines had not been formally involved in the operation in any capacity, so this was clearly a political move. The pilots themselves all came from good units, and the Officer appointed to oversee their training was a Marine Corps Colonel named Chuck Pittman.

Pittman quickly got down to the task in hand, his efficient methods and knowledge of helicopter operations impressed the Delta guys and they soon felt comfortable with him and his newly appointed team. The Marine pilots were based at the Yuma Army Airfield, and flew most of their training missions at night, they had a lot to learn and were putting in the flying hours. The transition period of changing helicopter platforms was managed successfully, even though some of them had never flown an RH-53D, or anything similar.

The real difficulty was developing and practising the new skills until they became second nature. These pilots had rarely flown at night, and on the occasions that they had it was always in near-perfect flight conditions. They were now being tasked with flying their helicopters at night, down narrow canyons, without lights and at very fast speeds; this tactic was developed to evade Radar and would play a key role in Iran. The pilots wore PVS5s night vision goggles to enable them to fly at night, however they could only be worn for thirty minutes at a time due to the fact that maps or instruments could not be read whilst wearing them. This meant that the pilot and co-pilot would have to constantly change roles to successfully manage the work-load.

It was considered that extra aircrew could be assigned to the operation to help with this work-load and the complicated navigation issues, however the cockpit of the RH-53D is cramped and there is little room for the pilots – let alone a dedicated navigator. Most helicopter missions are short in duration and the navigational issues are usually shared between the pilot and co-pilot, on this mission however an extra pilot would have been a welcome addition as success was imperative.

When planning an operation the numbers of personnel involved, and the number of helicopters needed to move them, had to be considered. The distance between the proposed mission departure point, in this case the Gulf of Oman and Desert One, was vast. If the Iranians discovered the rescue force before 'Eagle Claw' got into full swing, how quickly could they bring in reinforcements? Furthermore would they want to?

Colonel Beckwith knew that his Delta team were the best that America had to offer for such an operation, however they could not be expected to undertake impossible tasks. If too many personnel were used then the numbers of helicopters would have to go up, and with the problems that had already been faced with pilot training, they certainly did not need a demand for more aircrew.

A figure of 72 operators plus aircrews was put forward as a good number for such a mission, however it quickly became apparent that this was nowhere near enough and a revised figure of 120 was submitted. This new figure was based on intelligence gained regarding the exact location of the hostages within the Embassy compound. It was agreed that if the hostages were held in the chancellery of the compound, then an entire squadron alone would be needed to assault and secure it. The compound covered 27-acres and for Delta to seize it, the force would have to be subdivided into three sections. The force deployed on this operation comprised of two Squadrons, A and B; A Squadron and B Squadron were then broken down into smaller mission specific elements, known as *Red, Blue* and *White. Red* was essentially made up of A Squadron and was tasked with freeing the hostages held in the south-west quarter of the compound – this included the staff cottages and the commissary. *Red* were further tasked with securing the motor pool and power plant. If the Iranians decided to put up a flight, there was clearly going to be heavy casualties on both sides. The idea of a bloodless rescue had long since been seen as totally unrealistic and wishful thinking by the politicians. *Blue* element was composed of mainly B Squadron and was tasked with clearing and releasing the hostages held in the two residences – a warehouse known as the Mushroom, and the chancellery. *White* element was made up of operators taken from Selection and Training and from HQ staff. Their task was to support the assaulting forces, and to secure and hold the streets surrounding the compound.

Everyone realized that this was not going to be easy, the rehearsals went well within the embassy mock-up in Arizona, but the real operation was going to be something else. Now that the Delta Force team had been tasked, the number of helicopters needed could be determined. It was assessed that only six helicopters would be needed to carry the operators plus the rescued hostages, however it was agreed that due to the unreliable nature of helicopters, eight would be used in order to provide a good back-up. There were to be no dedicated gunships on the mission, as it was felt that the threat situation from ground based forces around Desert One would be minimal. The one weapon that the helicopter crews feared was the ZSU-23 Russian-built self-propelled AAA gun. This weapon posed a serious threat to both the helicopters and Delta on the ground. Capable of firing 6,000 rounds a minute they were lethal, and caused much concern to the planners because their locations were unknown. These weapons were mounted on a light armoured chassis, which was fitted with both target acquisition and tracking radar to direct the four 23mm cannons that were mounted on this weapon.

One possible method of destroying these weapons was to have two AC-130E/H gunships fly over Teheran as the operation went down. One would be tasked with flying top cover over the embassy, the other one would circle Mehrabad International Airport, where it was known that two F4 Phantoms were based – these could also pose a very serious threat.

One area of concern to Delta was the use of the AC-130E/H Gunship. If they had to call for fire-support in Teheran, there could be a danger of the support helicopters getting caught in the crossfire. This was one of the reasons that the use of helicopter gunships was rejected during the initial planning stage of the operation, as they cannot co-exist in a confined battle area, for fear of being hit by friendly forces.

By early March 1980, the planning for the operation was almost complete. The pilot training was going well under the command of Lieutenant Colonel Seiffert and confidence in their ability to pull this mission off was good. America had also planted an undercover agent in Teheran, who was able to feed good intelligence back to the JCS, via the CIA, on the daily developments in the Embassy. This was to be a key placement, having one man on the inside was worth a hundred men on the outside, and his ability to organize people within Iran was to prove significant.

Delta had also identified another area for them to hold up after they had met with the helicopters at Desert One. This area was to be known as 'Delta hide site' and was located at 35 14' N by 52 15' E. After dropping them off, the helicopters would proceed to their own hide fifteen miles north of Delta, in the hills around Garmsar. These new areas had been brought into the plan, due to the fact that the operation could not be carried out in one day. A place had to be designated for them to hide during daylight hours, before the rescue would be attempted after last light.

This part of the planning was very complicated, technically the operation should have been carried out over three days, however this was far too long for a force of this size to lay up without being discovered. It was agreed that the length of the operation would be two days, this would give Delta a night time arrival at Delta 1 to refuel the helicopters and load the operators, with a move to their hides under cover of darkness. They

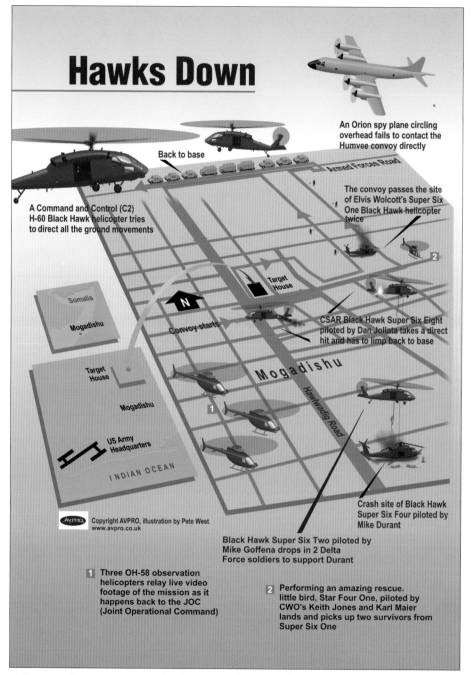

Hawks Down

An Orion spy plane circling overhead fails to contact the Humvee convoy directly

Back to base

The convoy passes the site of Elvis Wolcott's Super Six One Black Hawk helicopter twice

A Command and Control (C2) H-60 Black Hawk helicopter tries to direct all the ground movements

Armed Forces Road

2

Somalia

Mogadishu

Target House

N

Convoy starts

CSAR Black Hawk Super Six Eight piloted by Dan Jollata takes a direct hit and has to limp back to base

Target House

Mogadishu

M o g a d i s h u

Haviliwadig Road

1

US Army Headquarters

INDIAN OCEAN

Crash site of Black Hawk Super Six Four piloted by Mike Durant

AVPRO Copyright AVPRO, illustration by Pete West
www.avpro.co.uk

Black Hawk Super Six Two piloted by Mike Goffena drops in 2 Delta Force soldiers to support Durant

1 Three OH-58 observation helicopters relay live video footage of the mission as it happens back to the JOC (Joint Operational Command)

2 Performing an amazing rescue, little bird, Star Four One, piloted by CWO's Keith Jones and Karl Maier lands and picks up two survivors from Super Six One

A diagram showing the operation in Mogadishu, Somalia. (AVPRO)

US Rangers form a defensive perimeter around the wreckage of Elvis Wolcott's Black Hawk helicopter, after it was shot down by Somali gunmen during a raid on Mogadishu Warlords. (AVPRO)

A Black Hawk from the "Night Stalkers" lands back at its base, after a routine patrol over Mogadishu. (D. Oliver)

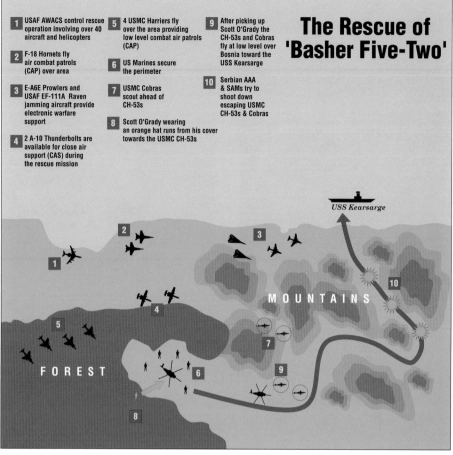

1. USAF AWACS control rescue operation involving over 40 aircraft and helicopters

2. F-18 Hornets fly air combat patrols (CAP) over area

3. E-A6E Prowlers and USAF EF-111A Raven jamming aircraft provide electronic warfare support

4. 2 A-10 Thunderbolts are available for close air support (CAS) during the rescue mission

5. 4 USMC Harriers fly over the area providing low level combat air patrols (CAP)

6. US Marines secure the perimeter

7. USMC Cobras scout ahead of CH-53s

8. Scott O'Grady wearing an orange hat runs from his cover towards the USMC CH-53s

9. After picking up Scott O'Grady the CH-53s and Cobras fly at low level over Bosnia toward the USS Kearsarge

10. Serbian AAA & SAMs try to shoot down escaping USMC CH-53s & Cobras

The Rescue of 'Basher Five-Two'

A diagram depicting the rescue of Capt. Scott O'Grady also known as 'Basher Five-Two.' (AVPRO)

A USAF MH-53J refuels in mid-air after carrying out humanitarian relief operations in Mozambique, Africa. Humanitarian operations have greatly increased in recent years and the sight of an MH-53 is always welcome by those in need. (USAF)

Capt. Scott O'Grady, better known as 'Basher Five-Two,' sets foot onboard the USS Kearsarge after being rescued by the US Marines, following his ordeal of being shot-down over Bosnia during a routine patrol. (D. Oliver)

An MH-53J shows off its impressive low-level performance during a routine training flight. (USAF)

This painting shows the dramatic rescue of F-16 pilot Capt. Scott O'Grady. (AVPRO)

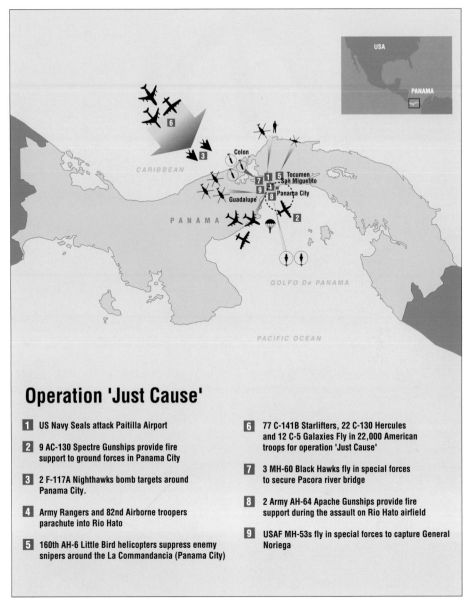

Operation 'Just Cause'

1   US Navy Seals attack Paitilla Airport

2   9 AC-130 Spectre Gunships provide fire support to ground forces in Panama City

3   2 F-117A Nighthawks bomb targets around Panama City.

4   Army Rangers and 82nd Airborne troopers parachute into Rio Hato

5   160th AH-6 Little Bird helicopters suppress enemy snipers around the La Commandancia (Panama City)

6   77 C-141B Starlifters, 22 C-130 Hercules and 12 C-5 Galaxies Fly in 22,000 American troops for operation 'Just Cause'

7   3 MH-60 Black Hawks fly in special forces to secure Pacora river bridge

8   2 Army AH-64 Apache Gunships provide fire support during the assault on Rio Hato airfield

9   USAF MH-53s fly in special forces to capture General Noriega

A diagram illustrating the positions of the aircraft that took part in Operation 'Just Cause.' (AVPRO)

USAF MH-53Js pictured here in Sarajevo, preparing for operations in the Balkans. (USAF)

The highly agile 'Little Bird' is a great asset to the Night Stalkers, as often demonstrated in conflicts such as Panama and Somalia. The pilots of these helicopters are amongst the best in the US Armed Forces. (160th SOAR)

Go ahead, make my day. A Night Stalkers Black Hawk hovers over a potential target. (160th SOAR)

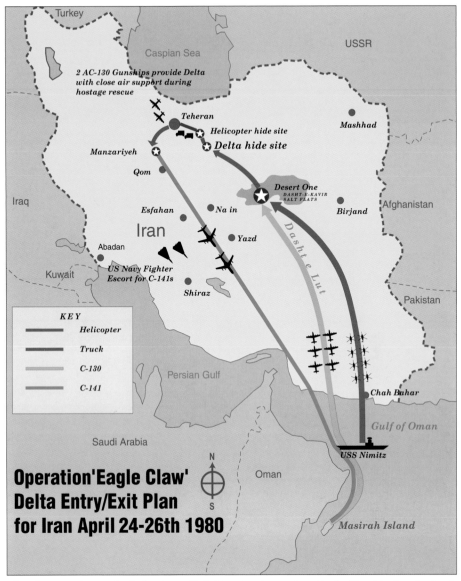

This diagram shows the Delta Entry/Exit Plan for Operation 'Eagle Claw' in Iran in April 1980. (AVPRO)

The morning after the night before. America's attempt to rescue hostages in Iran, is shattered after a collision between a Sea Stallion helicopter and a C-130 transport aircraft. (POPPERFOTO)

The moment when disaster struck Operation 'Eagle Claw' is captured in this dramatic painting by Ronald Wong. (AVPRO)

would hide up in the daylight hours and commence the rescue after last light. There were still details to be finalized, such as how Delta would get from its hides to Teheran. To use a helicopter would be too noisy and would alert the Embassy guards – making it very difficult, if not impossible, to surprise them.

The waiting during this period began to take its toll on the men, they were frustrated at having to train without any end in sight and wanted to know when the mission was going to go ahead. Beckwith held the British SAS view: *Train hard, Fight easy.* The longer the wait for Delta, the more their enemies in Iran would 'switch off'. They had, after all, held the hostages for more then four months without anything significant happening, so their guard would be down.

It was very cold in Teheran around this time of year, and intelligence had reported that the Iranian guards were not patrolling the streets around the Embassy as frequently as they had done earlier in the crisis. Instead they would gather around old oil drums that had been made into makeshift fires. This was good news for Delta as they would have a greater chance of taking the guards out while they were occupied keeping warm.

In late March 1980, Delta received news that the reconnaissance mission that they had requested to survey the Desert One site had been approved. The insertion of a small three-man team was to be carried out using a small Short Take-off and Landing (STOL) Aircraft operating from out of Egypt. The STOL team consisted of two pilots and an Air Force Major. Their mission was to collect rock and soil samples from the Desert One site, whilst taking photographs to verify the suitability of the area for air operations. They also surveyed a nearby road to monitor the level of traffic, and were seen by several occupants of a car, who probably assumed that they were Geologists surveying the local desert.

They also had another task to perform while they were there. Before gaining approval to fly the aircraft into the desert, much work had gone into developing a package of special aircraft landing lights, which were small enough to be carried aboard the STOL aircraft. These lights were then sited around the desert floor to mark out a landing strip. These could be turned on by remote control (from up to three miles away) from one of the C-130 aircraft as it approached the strip, which made them invisible at all other times. The mission was a complete success, and their expertly gained evidence confirmed the suitability of the strip for large aircraft such as the EC-130s, this was good news because it meant that the blivet concept could be discarded once and for all. Another idea to improve the plan was put forward by Colonel Kyle who suggested that instead of Delta flying in on helicopters from the *USS Nimitz*, they should fly in from Egypt with the C-130s and meet the helicopters at Desert One. This was soon incorporated into the mission. The team in situ in Teheran also solved another problem for Delta. They had put together a small fleet of vehicles to transport Delta from their hide site to the Embassy compound. At long last they now had all the pieces of the puzzle in place. The only thing remaining was to convince the US President, Jimmy Carter, that this operation was viable and could succeed. The following outline plan was put before President Carter and his advisory team.

OPERATION 'EAGLE CLAW'

The Code name of the operation to free American hostages held in Teheran will be 'Eagle Claw'. Three troop-carrying MC-130s and three fuel bearing EC-130s will depart from the Island of Masirah, located off the coast of Oman and fly to a location known as Desert One (33 05' N by 55 48'E). Upon landing, they will await the arrival of eight RH-53Ds, launching from the *USS Nimitz* in the Gulf of Oman. These will arrive in four sections, comprising of two helicopters per section, and arrive thirty minutes after the last C-130 has landed. On arrival they will refuel and on-load an assault force of 118 men. It will be critical to the operation, that a minimum of six RH-53Ds be serviceable to undertake the mission. In the event of this not being possible the operation will be terminated at Desert One, as this figure is the lowest permitted by the Air Planners to carry both personnel and equipment to the next location. After refuelling and on-loading Delta the helicopters are to proceed to the following location at 35 14'N by 52 15'E. This will be known as Delta hide-site. The aircraft that supported the operation at Desert One will return to Masirah. After unloading Delta and their equipment, the helicopters will fly to their own hide-site located some fifteen miles north of Delta. All elements of the move, will take place in darkness with all forces to be in place within their hides before day-break. There will be no move before sundown on this day.

At Delta's landing zone there will be two DoD (Department of Defence) agents there to meet them and lead them on a five-mile overland walk to their hide-site, a remote Wadi located some sixty-five miles south-east of Teheran. After last light, the two DoD agents will return with two vehicles, a Datsun pickup truck and a Volkswagen bus. The vehicles will transport six drivers and six translators to the outskirts of Teheran with Colonel Beckwith, the mission commander. They will pick up six enclosed Mercedes trucks that are stored within a warehouse, and return to Delta's hide. During this time Colonel Beckwith will carry out a reconnaissance of the Embassy and return to Delta's hide-site upon completion.

At 2030 hours Delta will board the vehicles in three sections, *Red*, *White* and *Blue*, each section will be given different tasks to accomplish during the rescue. The first stage of the ground mission will be to drive along the Damavand road in a northerly direction through two checkpoints, one at Eyvanekey, the other at Sherifabad. If Delta are compromised at this stage they will seize the guards and take them prisoner.

The journey to the Embassy will be decided on the day, based upon the reconnaissance carried out by Colonel Beckwith and the DoD agents. The best case scenario would be for a vehicle to drive ahead of the convoy as a scout car, reporting on possible problems and re-directing the convoy as required, should this prove necessary. A thirteen-man assault team will be tasked with the rescue of three hostages, known to be held in the Foreign Ministry Building. They will use the Volkswagen bus and travel by a different route to the target building. Between 2300 hours and midnight a small team of operators will drive up to the Embassy using the Datsun pickup. They will take out all the guards at the main entrance and in Roosevelt Avenue using guns fitted with silencers.

Once the guards have been neutralized, *Red*, *White* and *Blue* section will move towards the Embassy in the trucks, driving in two abreast formation. When they arrive in Roosevelt Avenue they will climb over the Embassy wall by means of ladders. *Red* section, comprising of forty men, will be responsible for securing the western sector of the compound. They will free any hostages found in the staff cottages and the commissary. They are further tasked to neutralize any guards in the motor pool and power plant areas. *Blue* section, consisting of forty men, will be responsible for securing the Embassy's eastern sector. They will free any hostages found in the Deputy Chief of Commission's residence, the Ambassador's residence, the Mushroom, and the Chancellery. *White* section is the smallest unit with only 13 men, its role will be to secure Roosevelt Avenue and set up a defensive position to cover the withdrawal of *Red* and *Blue* sections. It will be equipped with two heavy machine guns to provide fire support if required.

Air support will be provided by two AC-130 gunships on station over Teheran, their role will be to prevent reinforcements from reaching the Embassy and to ensure that no Iranian fighter aircraft become airborne from the local airport, as they could present a serious threat to the rescue helicopters.

The signal to initiate the assault will be the demolition of the Embassy compound wall by Red section. This will be a large explosion, and will instantly alert the guards. Any who provide resistance will be killed by Delta. The hostages will be gathered together and taken to the compound grounds and await helicopter arrival, the RH-53Ds will be orbiting north of the city and will come in on a signal given by Delta's air-operations officer. The compound has a number of poles inserted to prevent helicopter landings, if these cannot be brought down by demolition charges, then Delta will evacuate all forces and hostages via the nearby Soccer stadium. Any hostages requiring medical attention will be treated by Delta's medics.

It is anticipated that the mission will take less than one hour to accomplish, taking into account any resistance and time spent clearing rooms to ensure no hostages are left behind. As this operation is taking place a team of Rangers will fly into Manzariyeh airfield, their mission being to take and secure the airfield, pending the arrival of Delta from Teheran thirty-five miles north. Once all operators have arrived in Manzariyeh, they will be airlifted out by C-141 Starlifters. This extraction will include all hostages, drivers, DoD agents, helicopter pilots, drivers, translators and Delta operators. The Rangers will withdraw after everyone else on a separate aircraft. Should any helicopters become unserviceable or damaged due to enemy action, a shuttle operation will take place until everyone is evacuated. In the event that helicopter operations are not possible, Delta will use the vehicles that they have to escape and evade capture by heading north-west towards Turkey. This concludes Delta Forces' hostage rescue plan Operation 'Eagle Claw.'

The members of the Department of Defence and the White House who attended the Delta briefing were impressed with what they had heard, and made a recommendation to President Carter to give approval for Operation 'Eagle Claw'. During the months of February and March there had been much debate over the rules of engagement. This had to be resolved and a clear understanding had to be agreed for Delta, to enable them to operate with an Official mandate. The last thing that anybody wanted was a situation like Vietnam, where politicians interfered constantly with military operations causing confusion and loss of momentum in the operational planning of missions. Once President Carter gave the go ahead 'Eagle Claw' would be underway and the mission would either succeed or fail.

President Carter had thought long and hard about his decision, he had exhausted all political options and the only option left was the military solution. The operation that he had in mind would be 'quick, incisive, surgical and without loss of American lives', Operation 'Eagle Claw' was about the best that he was going to get. The thought of failure didn't bear thinking about, he had relived the nightmare of failure over and over again, the thoughts of what the Iranians would do to the American hostages should this operation fail were almost too much to contemplate. He had to give the order, as it was the only card on the table that hadn't been played.

In April, President Carter summoned the mission commanders, and informed them that he wished to speak with them at the White House. There was a feeling that somehow this meeting was going to be different, the venue gave something of a clue that this was not to be a normal routine briefing. Over the last five months there had been countless meetings and briefings involving the DoD and JCS with no end in sight, the briefing on 16 April was with President Carter and the National Security Council. This now seemed real.

Colonel Beckwith attended this meeting with General Vaught and General Gast, they were taken to a small room within the White House where they were met by Hamilton Jordan, the chief of staff for the White House. The room they were in was known as The Situation Room, this was the inner sanctum, the heart of America at this time. Also present in the room was Warren Christopher – the Deputy Secretary of State, Cyrus Vance, Dr Zbigniew Brzezinski – the President's National Security Advisor, along with Dr Brown – the Secretary of Defence accompanied by various people from his Office. This was America's military and political power-base all gathered together in one room, Vice President Mondale and President Jimmy Carter arrived in the room, and everyone took their seat. This was to be Judgement Day.

The military commanders each took their turn to present Operation 'Eagle Claw' to the highly attentive audience, every word was analyzed, each graphic studied, and they had dozens of questions for the speakers. The presentation was the same as earlier that day to the JCS, they had been impressed, and had approved it to the White House, hence the meeting with President Carter and his aides. President Carter followed every word of the mission commanders' and was clearly reassured with what they had to say. Every now and then, a member of the White House team would interrupt the speaker and ask for clarification of a point or detail. One of the questions put forward asked whether Delta were really going to kill the Iranian guards in the embassy compound. The answer was 'yes'. This shocked some of the people in the room, however most knew it was the only way that an operation like this could succeed.

Another question was how the guards were to be differentiated from the hostages as the guards wore the same western clothes as the hostages. The answer was that anyone who held a gun would be deemed a guard and would be shot, those that were clearly Americans would be given Yellow arm bands and escorted from the compound by Delta.

However, there was still one fear that Delta had; it was often possible during long hostage incidents for prisoners and guards to develop relationships, where during a rescue they have been known to jump into the line of fire to protect their captors from being shot. Psychologists had advised Delta of such cases, and advised them to be on their guard, so they were well prepared for this. Another fear was that there were several hostages that had military backgrounds, and on hearing Delta assault the building they may try to overpower the guards and take their weapons. These were the ones that presented Delta with the most concern, because the assault team would be under great stress during the initial attack and anyone running around with a gun, be they American or Iranian, would be presumed hostile and shot dead.

After the formal briefing had concluded, President Carter asked the key question. "How many casualties, do you see here?" This question was answered by General Vaught, he stated that he did not honestly know, but thought the figure of seven Delta operators and three hostages wounded seemed a realistic possibility. One area of 'Eagle Claw' that was still open and unresolved, related to the provision of TACAIR (Tactical Air Support). There would be two AC-130s over Teheran protecting Delta on the ground, however against Iranian jet fighters they would be useless. The C-141s leaving Manzariyeh with Delta, the hostages and the Rangers, also had no protection from air attack. It would be a disaster if America pulled off a spectacular rescue mission only to have the transport aircraft shot down on the way home. President Carter dealt with this issue in one sentence. "There will be air cover from Manzariyeh all the way out of Iran." Problem solved.

A member of the group then asked the President, "Mr President, my agency now needs to know what your decision will be. Should we move forward and pre-position?"
The President calmly responded, "It's time for me to summarise. I do not want to undertake this operation, but we have no other recourse. The only way I will call it off now is if the International Red Cross hands back our Americans . . . We're going to do this operation".

This was the answer that everyone had been waiting for,

straight from the horse's mouth. It was on. The dates for the operation had been decided. On 24 April, Delta would enter Iran, 25 April they would hide up during the day and commence the rescue that night and in the early hours of 26 April, they would leave Iran and head for home.

During the meeting President Carter decided on the communication line. It was to be as simple as possible, It would be a military operation so General Jones would run it, his only two reporting contacts, the Secretary of Defence, Dr Brown and the President, Jimmy Carter. Nobody else in that room was to be involved. This was a milestone in American history and President Carter had taken a brave decision. Before everyone left the room, President Carter called Colonel Beckwith to one side and stated,

"I want to ask you to do two things for me, I want you, before you leave for Iran, to assemble all of your force and when you think it's appropriate give them a message from me. Tell them that in the event this operation fails, for whatever reason, the fault will not be theirs, it will be mine. And the second thing is, if any American is killed, hostage or Delta Force, if it is possible – as long as it doesn't jeopardize the life of someone else, you bring the body back." Colonel Beckwith promised the President that he would comply with his wishes, and knew that when, he left the White House that night, one way or another he was going down in history.

Colonel Beckwith returned to Delta's base at Fort Bragg to prepare his men for the long flight to Egypt via Frankfurt, Germany. As far as anyone else on the base was concerned they were just getting ready for yet another exercise, even Delta had not been told that the mission was live. In the early hours of Sunday morning on the 20 April 1980, Colonel Beckwith gathered his men together and informed them that they were going to Iran, this was no drill. He relayed President Carter's thoughts to them and they were extremely grateful for his words, at this time so little meant so much. Delta moved by truck to Pope Air Force Base and boarded two C-141s for the first stage of their journey to Frankfurt. On arrival at Frankfurt they picked up thirteen new passengers. The men they picked up were members of an elite American Special Forces unit based in Germany. Their mission was to accompany Delta and rescue three American hostages being held in the Ministry of Foreign Affairs building, which was close to the Embassy compound.

The reason for picking this team was due to the fact that Delta simply did not have enough men in their organization for such a large operation. The mission now numbered 132 men: 2 Iranian generals; 12 drivers; a 12-man road watch team to secure the road by Desert One; the 13-man Special Forces assault team; plus Delta's 93 operators and staff. The road watch team had the task of securing the road that ran alongside Desert One. Air based intelligence had confirmed that this was a little used highway, however it was still active so it was necessary to bring a small team in to secure it. Once this part of the operation was complete, the road team would board one of the C-130s and return to Egypt.

On Monday 21 April, the C-141s arrived at Wadi Kena, Egypt. The operators were tired from the long flight and mission nerves were starting to kick in. The location in Egypt was in a poor state, but it gave Delta a period to adjust to local time differences, and to catch up on rest. Delta set up a make-shift range to test-fire its weapons, and used the time in Egypt to sharpen weapon skills, knowing that the next time it would be for real. The Base was barely tolerable, the heat during the day and night made it hard to sleep as there was no air-conditioning; it had originally been built by the Russians for the Egyptians and was of poor quality. The only reason it was bearable was down to the hard work of an advance party that had cleaned it up before Delta had arrived. The base was a hive of activity, with Delta carrying out daily work routines to keep up fitness levels and constant rehearsals to keep their edge. The longer they stayed here the more their metabolism accustomed from daytime to night time. Their confidence and morale were high and they were keen to commence the rescue.

During Delta's stay in Egypt, news reached them that the hostages were being held in the Chancellery, so there needed to be a slight modification to the plan. *Blue* section would now have more security responsibilities – its main role now would be to neutralize the guards quarters, along with the motor pool and power plant. *Red* section would now concentrate its entire effort on assaulting the Chancellery. The level of guards in this build-ing would now be higher, so the mission would be even tougher than before. The plan would now be for a small *Red* team to force the staff door at the east of the building. When complete they would clear the central corridor and open the main entrance door that faced south, the main Red force would then enter the building and begin to clear the rooms.

In the early hours of Thursday 24 April, Delta left Egypt for the Island of Masirah off the coast of Oman. As the C-141s landed, they noticed the MC-130s and EC-130s parked on the apron awaiting their mission. Everything suddenly became very real, and seemed far-removed from all the talk and speculation. At 1630 hours, Delta started to board their aircraft. They dispensed with normal military uniforms, and wore dyed-Black military jackets, jeans and woollen skull-caps. On their jackets they wore a small American flag, which was covered with tape, as the mission started this was to be removed.

The Delta team was extremely well armed with M-16s, grenades, M40s and HK21s. Some of them brought personal favourite weapons in addition to their issued ones, and in sheer fire-power terms they outgunned the Iranian guards at the Embassy. At 1800 hours the first MC-130 took off with Colonel Beckwith, the Road Watch Team, the Combat Control Team and *Blue* section, they would provide the advance element to protect the location at Desert One in addition to establishing a communications net. The other five aircraft took off at slight intervals one hour later; this was to prevent attracting too much attention from ships in the Gulf of Oman. Russian spy ships were very active in the Gulf at this time so an air of normality had to be maintained.

The aircraft after take-off climbed and crossed the Gulf of Oman heading towards Iran. As they approached the Iranian coastline they descended to below five hundred feet to avoid detection by Iranian radar. Although their capability had dropped after the fall of the Shah, they still possessed modern radar systems that were highly sophisticated and remained operational. The MC-130s and EC-130s crossed the Iranian coastline west of Chah Bahar and headed for Desert One. In front of the pilots lay hills and mountains that would provide good cover for flying under the Iranian ground-based radar tracking system.

The Air Force had analyzed all the potential Radar traps, and plotted a course that would avoid them; this meant that the aircraft had to constantly lurch hard to port and starboard to avoid being detected. Flying nap of the earth (NOE) can be hard on the stomach, and several of the passengers became airsick during the flight. There was very little conversation from the members of

Delta; everyone had things on their mind, the mission, family at home, girlfriends and a thousand other reasons for not being on this mission. The cabin interior was lit only with small red lights to help prepare night vision – otherwise it would take an average eye forty-five minutes to adjust fully. They were going to hit the ground running, and as soon as they landed they would be out taking up their positions, there would be no time for delay. As the lead aircraft carrying Colonel Beckwith crossed the halfway point, news reached him that the eight RH-53D Sea Stallions had taken off from the *USS Nimitz* and were on their way to Desert One. This news brought a smile to his face – it was a proud moment for him. He had set Delta up from nothing and today he was leading 120 of America's finest soldiers into battle.

As Colonel Beckwith pressed on with his part of the mission, the last of the RH-53D Sea Stallions were leaving the deck of the *USS Nimitz* bound for Desert One. The helicopters had taken off in four sections, comprising of two helicopters per section. They had departed at staggered intervals to prevent bunching up on route, and each section had been given a different route to mini-mise detection by Iranian ground forces. The USMC pilots were glad to be airborne after spending so much time aboard the *Nimitz*. For security reasons the RH-53Ds had been hangared below deck for most of the journey, this was due to the fact that had Soviet Intelligence detected so many Sea Stallions parked on the deck of the *USS Nimitz*, it would have aroused too much interest. These RH-53Ds had been especially modified for the mission and Soviet photo interpreters would have spotted that all of their mine-detection equipment had been removed, apart from the rear supports. In addition they were fitted with extra fuel tanks for the mission ahead. As fuel was a critical factor in this operation the extra two hundred miles range provided by

these extra tanks was greatly welcomed. The particular helicopters used in this operation had been drawn from a fleet
of thirty such models operated by the US Navy; they had been
built around the mid-seventies, so in military terms they were
relatively new.

The USS Nimitz provided two of the RH-53Ds from its own
fleet, the other six came from the USS Kitty Hawk, which had
been on station in the Indian Ocean. The Nimitz was due to
replace Kitty Hawk as part of normal operational rotation, so
this part of the operation never attracted any attention from the
Russians. The helicopters in this operation were led by Colonel
Seiffert of the USMC. He had worked hard over the last few
months on training the USMC pilots for this mission and, like
Colonel Beckwith, he was proud of the role his men would play.

As with the MC-130s and EC-130s that had left Masirah earlier in the day, the helicopters would cross the Iranian coastline
west of Chah Bahar and proceed at low level over the barren
Iranian territory towards Desert One. For the USMC pilots flying this mission, this was the most challenging flying they had
ever done in their lives. The normal mission profiles undertaken
by the USMC were short in length and normally undertaken during daylight hours, this was way beyond what a normal Marine
pilot would be expected to do.

As Colonel Seiffert's crews proceeded with the mission,
everything seemed to be going well. The weather for the mission
was predicted as being clear all the way to Desert One, and so
far the Air Force had been one hundred percent right. Their
Satellite based reports were the best in the US Armed Forces,
however there were certain conditions that could not be predicted or detected quickly from above, and one of them was
about to hit the helicopter force hard.

Ahead of the lead helicopter there seemed to be a giant wall of cloud rising from the ground upwards for several thousand feet. The pilots at first thought it was low level cloud, such as that often seen off the coast – normally referred to as sea mist or sea fog. However this seemed strange, as they were hundreds of miles inland. What the helicopter crews were about to fly into was a condition known locally as a *haboob*. These are giant clouds of sand and dust that can reach several thousand feet in height, and can occupy a front many miles wide. Nothing can fully prepare a pilot for these conditions.

Because of the perceived threat from Iranian radar, the helicopter crews were flying only fifty feet above the ground, therefore they had no margin for error, just one mistake and they would hit the deck. With a *haboob* the sand clouds are thickest nearest to the ground, so the USMC pilots were getting the worst of it since they had been ordered to fly at such a low altitude. One of the pilots later described his experience of flying through the *haboob*, as being like flying in a bowl of milk. He was referring to the fact that visibility was down to zero, even with the night vision goggles on. Panic started to take its effect and they realised there were only three choices.

1. They could fly at a higher altitude to avoid the *haboob*, but then they would be picked up by Iranian radar and the mission would be compromised.
2. They could land the helicopters and ride out the storm, but then they faced two major problems. The first would be that the whole timing of the mission would be thrown out and the timing was critical for success. The next problem for the crews, was how they would start the engines of the helicopters – these helicopters required ground based systems to

crank them, but out here there was no such support. They had been given compressed air cylinders to fire the engines at Desert One, but these were very small, and wouldn't be enough to keep re-starting the engines.

3. The first two choices were out, so they were left with only one – to continue.

Another effect of the *haboob* was that when sand grains hit the rotor blades they would give off sparks; with the pilots wearing night vision goggles these effects were amplified and very unnerving to the pilots, who had never seen anything like this before. The workload on the pilots was intolerable, not only did they have to drag every ounce of flying skill out of themselves to keep the helicopters flying, they also had to navigate without seeing anything as a point of reference. It was not USMC doctrine to carry a dedicated navigator, as their missions were of a short nature and therefore a pilot could easily cope with both roles. Out here it was different, there was nobody else to share the load and they would have to carry on as best they could.

There were also further problems the pilots had to contend with. Before they had left training, the pilots had a totally new navigation system pushed on them called PINS (Palletized Inertial Navigation System). This was to be an alternative system to the familiar Omega system that they had previously been using, and at this late in the day their confidence was with Omega rather than PINS. The PINS system was said to be state of the art, and instructors who tried to teach the USMC pilots how to use it, felt that their hearts and soul were never really into learning it as they had become used to Omega. The pilots battled on through the haboob however, wondering when would it end, and how their colleagues were coping.

Meanwhile, about three miles from Desert One, Colonel Beckwith's MC-130 was approaching the remote site and lining up for a landing, the pilot switched on the remote-controlled lights that had been planted by the STOL team and they glowed faintly in the distance. The pilot flew one circle over the LZ before landing in an east to west direction.

The landing was smooth and the STOL recce team's effort to survey the LZ had clearly been of great benefit to Delta. It was now 2200 hours and everything at Desert One was looking good. As the MC-130 parked up, the rear ramp lowered and the Road Watch Team made up of Rangers and Delta left the aircraft to take up their positions on the sites' flanks. They had motorcycles and a quarter-ton jeep for mobility to patrol the extensive site. The teams had barely left the aircraft for their positions, when they saw a large Mercedes bus driving towards them with its headlights on full-beam. Colonel Beckwith shouted at the Rangers to stop the vehicle and this they did by firing at the bus. It braked hard and came to a sudden halt near *Blue* section, who had just got off the plane. They quickly surrounded it and ordered the passengers off. In all there were 45 people on board, mainly elderly folks with some young children; they were ordered to stand near the side of the road where they were searched and placed under close guard.

They could have done without this complication so early in the operation, but it was a factor that had been taken into consideration during the planning. They planned to put them on a C-130, fly them out to Masirah and return them the next night to Manzariyeh. After the initial excitement of stopping the bus, the remainder of the Road Watch Team made their way towards the western end of the LZ to set up a road block. As they moved into position a large gasoline tanker appeared on the road ahead of them, driving in an erratic manner at very high speed. Captain Wade Ishimoto, Delta's intelligence officer was standing by the road block with a Ranger from the Road Watch Team and attempted to stop the vehicle by standing in the middle of the road with his hand in the air. The driver of the truck could clearly see the road block yet refused to stop, even with Ishimoto in the way – he had no intention of stopping for anyone. Captain Ishimoto opened fire on the vehicle with his M-16, but failed to stop it, he shouted at the Ranger nearby to take the truck out with his M72 LAW (Light Antitank Weapon). This he did with spectacular results, the projectile hit the truck and caused a tremendous explosion that lit up the skies for miles around They had hit a 5000 gallon fuel truck, which was fully loaded.

Captain Ishimoto raced towards the truck but before he got to it, the driver jumped out and ran away. At this point a second vehicle drove up behind the burning truck and picked up the driver that had just escaped. Before they could react the vehicle sped off into the darkness down another track away from the LZ. Captain Ishimoto tried to give chase, however his motor-bike failed to start; by the time it fired up it was too late and they were long gone.

Colonel Beckwith believed that they were gasoline smugglers and probably thought the road block was manned by Iranian Police. In any case he doubted if they had seen the MC-130 on the ground, even though the visibility that night was good. Colonel Beckwith decided that these incidents were not serious enough to warrant terminating the operation at this stage. Even if the drivers of the trucks informed the Iranian Police, which was highly unlikely, it is doubtful that they would have been believed. So he decided that if any more vehicles came along the road he would set up a parking lot for them, as he had seen more traffic in one hour on the local road, than the Satellites had picked up in a day. Everything else on Desert One had now been set up including the Combat Control Team, which was responsible for air traffic operations.

The C-130 that had dropped Colonel Beckwith and his team off was now ready for take-off back to Masirah. It received permission and roared down the makeshift runway leaving the small ground team feeling a little vulnerable as it climbed into the night sky. The aircraft had barely departed, when the sound of another C-130 could be heard as it approached Desert One to make a landing. The pilots of the C-130 were expecting to land in pitch-black conditions. Instead they could clearly see the gasoline truck, which was still burning fiercely with flames reaching 300 feet into the sky. Once the aircraft landed it was quickly unloaded of its cargo of camouflage netting which was there to cover the eight helicopters the following day. Over the next hour the remainder of the aircraft arrived and discharged their cargoes of equipment and operators. The fuel laden EC-130s were positioned north to south in a long line with a large gap between each aircraft for safety reasons, and to allow room for the helicopters to refuel after landing.

At this time Desert One was a scene of intense activity with operators moving equipment from aircraft to their various sections awaiting the arrival of the helicopters. As they moved about another C-130 took off bound for Masirah. The aircraft movements were extremely efficient and on time and many of the pilots commented that the real operation was running more smoothly than the rehearsals – the only concern now was the helicopters. They were now overdue and Colonel Beckwith was getting impatient. There was no way of communicating with them by radio, and the Delta operators were becoming edgy.

During rehearsals they had worked with a ten-minute tolerance, now over thirty minutes had gone by and there was nothing. The main problem they faced was that by the time the helicopters refuelled and loaded up Delta, dawn would be breaking and they would be in the open.

Contact had been made with the agents in Teheran and Delta hide site, they were now aware of the situation at Desert One. Colonel Beckwith was anxiously walking up and down the LZ, asking where the helicopters were. He was unaware that his USMC pilots and their eight Sea Stallion helicopters were battling against the worst flying conditions imaginable. Where he was at Desert One, the sky was clear and visibility excellent, where they were the sky was full of sand and dust with terrible visibility. This part of the operation was now in dire straits, the pilots knew how important it was to be at Desert One on time but they could do nothing; the cockpits of the Sea Stallions were filling with choking sand and dust from the *haboob*, making breathing very difficult. They were all mentally and physically exhausted and most of them thought that they would never survive this ordeal, especially at such a low altitude. Another problem was since the helicopters were optimised for maritime operations, not Desert, they had not been fitted with sand filters or the correct lubricants, as a result the engine intakes were filling up with sand. This in turn had its effect on the engines, if air cannot reach an engine then it loses power and starts to overheat and as a result the helicopter will fly slower, therefore using more fuel.

The helicopters and Marine pilots were being pushed beyond their limits, and something had to give. The first flight emergency had now developed, helicopter number six had serious problems with its rotors and the pilots were struggling to keep it airborne.

There was no alternative but to land, they signalled to helicopter number eight that they were in trouble and would be making an emergency landing. They gently flared the helicopter and brought it down safely without any injuries to the crew. On the ground the sand and dust was swirling around everywhere, making it difficult to see each member of the crew let alone the other helicopter. With great flying skills the other pilot landed and picked them up, they were one down already and there was still a long way to go to Desert One.

The Sea Stallion lifted off the ground with its extra passengers and tried to increase its speed to make up for lost time. The helicopter emerged from the *haboob* briefly, only to find another one waiting to take its place. This *haboob* was even worse than the first one. Its density was much greater and caused the temperature to rise dramatically in the cockpit. All the helicopters were now having problems – especially number five. Throughout the flight their instrumentation had been malfunctioning, and with only the altimeter and compass to rely on they were facing serious problems. It was impossible for them to see out of the cockpit windows, due to the intense sand and dust – as a consequence visual navigation was impossible. The other problem was the altitude at which they were flying. Under normal circumstances flying fifty feet above the ground at night and at high speed would be highly dangerous, but with no altimeter and no means of seeing where they were going it was conditions were approaching suicidal.

The Captain of Sea Stallion five had made his mind up. He was turning back for the *USS Nimitz*. It would have been foolish for him to continue to Desert One; his duty as a USMC Officer was to protect the lives of his fellow crewmembers, and this he did.

'Eagle Claw' was now down to six helicopters. It seemed that all the latent fears that everyone had harboured about the helicopters were coming true. They had always had a reputation for unreliability, but with the dedication of the support crews these helicopters had been able to operate during the training missions without any degree of problems. This mission was just too much for man and machine, and time was running out.

Ahead of the lead helicopter at Desert One, Colonel Beckwith was shouting at his fellow officers for information on the helicopters, just as he was about to give up on them he heard the familiar and welcome whooping sound of a Sea Stallion in the distance. As the first helicopter came into land another one was picked up on the radio, its ETA only minutes away from the LZ. Shortly after the first helicopter had landed, Colonel Beckwith walked up to the cockpit of the Sea Stallion to greet the crew. He was taken somewhat by surprise when he spoke to the pilot, Major James Schaefer. He looked shattered, and said that his flight had been hell, he told Colonel Beckwith that he should order the operators back onto the aircraft and terminate the mission here and now as it was falling apart. Colonel Beckwith reassured him that everything would be fine and that he should relax, as the mission was still on, even if they arrived in the hide-sites during daylight.

As they talked, the second helicopter came into view and landed nearby. Over the next hour the other four helicopters arrived at staggered intervals over Desert One. The ground operators were amazed at the fact that no two helicopters arrived from the same direction, all arriving over the LZ from different points of the compass. As they landed they were marshalled towards the waiting EC-130s for refuelling and loading. The operators commented on the fact that the pilots all looked terrible, it was evident that they had been through an ordeal.

One of the last helicopters to arrive brought Colonel Seiffert, the USMC Officer in charge of air operations. On landing he demanded to speak with Colonel Beckwith. At their meeting, Beckwith was shocked at what he heard regarding the pilots' journey in, they were openly stating that the operation should be terminated at once. They had already lost two helicopters, and the operation could only be carried out with a minimum of six. Seiffert had seen at first hand how the men and helicopters were coping with this mission and his view was that they were likely to lose another helicopter before the rescue team went in. He urged Beckwith to reconsider his position as they could always return a few weeks later and try again. The feelings amongst the operators were that the USMC pilots were looking for a way out, although they didn't really appreciate what the pilots had gone through, and that for them to even make it to Desert One was a major achievement.

There was clearly a crisis at Desert One now. Delta wanted to just get on with the job and were becoming impatient with the USMC pilots who were asking for the operation to be terminated. Colonel Beckwith wanted his men and equipment loaded on the Sea Stallions as soon as possible and was putting pressure on Colonel Seiffert to move quickly. It was a very busy scene, with six helicopters and four aircraft on the ground all with engines running. The noise was deafening and the air was filled with sand and dust kicked up from the aircraft and helicopters, making conversation very hard. The men moved through the LZ taking their positions up behind designated helicopters, according to which section they had been assigned to. The operation was now over ninety minutes behind schedule, and tempers were fraying.

There was a lot of tension between Colonel Seiffert and Colonel Beckwith at this time. Both men were responsible for many peoples' lives and the stress was beginning to tell. As Beckwith supervised the loadings, a pilot informed him that helicopter number two had hydraulic problems and couldn't fly. This was the final straw, how could they perform the mission with only five helicopters? The set rules were that the absolute minimum would be six. These numbers had already been set by air operations taking into account Delta, the hostages and other personnel and their total weights.

By now General Vaught had stepped into the discussion asking Colonel Beckwith to consider going in with five helicopters only. Beckwith was furious, the golden rule he had learned in the British SAS was that if you make a plan, you stick with it or cancel the mission. All of the Delta operators had rehearsed this mission for five months, and for them to change it in five minutes was ludicrous. As embarrassing as it would be to cancel the operation at Desert One, it was far better then going into Teheran and risking Disaster with a half-baked plan. There was no way that the mission could go ahead with less men, everyone had their job and knew their specific role and at this stage it was too late to change.

Beckwith called together all the pilots and informed them that the operation was to be terminated with immediate effect. Delta was to be off loaded from the helicopters and put back on the C-130 and the EC-130s. The helicopters would return to the USS Nimitz and maybe in a few weeks time they would make another attempt. Before they all left Desert One, the helicopters would have to be topped up with extra fuel as some of them had their engines running for over an hour and would need that fuel to get them back to the Nimitz. There was no question of leaving the working helicopters behind for the Iranians; they would however blow up helicopter number two, as this was deemed too risky to fly.

Beckwith was still angry from the earlier telephone call on the Sat-phone with General Vaught. He couldn't believe what they had asked him to do, here he was standing in the middle of a desert with aircraft and helicopters around him with chaos reigning supreme and they wanted him to carry on. He had now lost three helicopters and in the background the gasoline truck was still burning. At this moment there were four helicopters parked north of the highway behind some of the C-130s, while to the south the other two had taken up position behind the other transports. Colonel Kyle gave the order for the other helicopters to prepare to move back to the USS *Nimitz*, once helicopter four had finished refuelling. Major Schaeffer was in helicopter number three and moved aside to allow number four to pass, as he did a sudden gust of wind caught the helicopter and lifted it up into the air, causing it to land on top of the nearby C-130 transport aircraft with devastating results. The rotors had cut through the cockpit and fractured a fuel tank, there was an explosion followed by a massive fireball, which sent flames over 300 feet into the night sky. The flames were getting close to the other parked aircraft and men were running out of the burning C-130 in sheer panic in all directions. The ammunition and ground-to-air missiles aboard the aircraft and helicopter started to 'cook off'. There seemed to be lead flying everywhere and some of the Redeye surface-to-air missiles flew through the air like fireworks.

The Sea Stallion had landed on top of the port fuselage and wing section of the C-130, and resembled a locust on top of its prey. It was a sickening site for everyone concerned and a miracle that so many people got out alive from the burning inferno. The smell of aviation fuel lingered in the air, and there was a serious threat of secondary explosions. Eight American servicemen perished in the crash with a further five seriously injured. Were it not for the heroic efforts of a couple of the men aboard the C-130, who risked their own lives going back into the inferno to rescue others, many more would have died. During the panic to leave the aircraft, many secret files and documents were left behind along with weapons and equipment, many of which were found by the Iranians later in the day.

The scene at Desert One was now one of chaos. Delta Operators were dragging their injured colleagues away from the burning C-130 and helicopter, everyone was looking around for leadership and direction. In any crisis situation a poor decision is better then no decision and there was only one option. Get out fast. The order was given to abandon the helicopters, the USMC pilots were ordered to board the C-130s as quickly as possible, due to the urgency to leave the Desert One LZ. Colonel Beckwith had given orders for the Sea Stallions to be blown up before they left – however this did not happen. One of the Operators had raised General Vaught on the radio and requested an air-strike on Desert One to destroy the helicopters and the Delta support equipment. This was to be an alternative action to ground forces remaining behind and performing the order, at great danger to themselves. As the C-130s roared off down the LZ one of the aircraft hit an embankment and nearly crashed. The crew immediately reacted to the incident by applying more power as the aircraft bounced on the ground. With the increased lift, the crew managed to coax the aircraft off the ground and kept it airborne.

As the last of the C-130s climbed into the dark Iranian sky,

Colonel Beckwith looked back at the scene of disaster at Desert One below. A Red glow could be seen on the ground, where the remains of the C-130 and Sea Stallion were, along with a small fire nearby which was the burning gasoline truck. It was a nightmare that they were glad to see the back of. Colonel Beckwith's thoughts were with the families of those that had been tragically killed. He thought of the promise that he had given to President Carter, that in the event of any American deaths, he would bring the bodies home. This was one promise that he just could not keep.

During the flight, word reached Beckwith that the request for an air-strike on the abandoned helicopters at Desert One had been denied. This was due to the fact that Iranian citizens were still on the bus near the site, and there was a high probability that an air-strike, no matter how precise, could kill them. If this happened the Iranian students holding the American hostages would have killed them as an act of revenge. Losing the helicopters would be a small price to pay compared to any more Americans losing their lives, as there had been enough blood-shed already.

The Delta Operators flew back to Masirah feeling frustrated, angry and extremely miserable, all of the training and rehearsals had come to nothing. America's hostage rescue operation lay in pieces on the desert floor far behind them now, yet the recriminations of this operation would live on for years to come. They eventually arrived in Egypt with Colonel Beckwith, at the base where the operation had all begun. They had barely landed when Colonel Beckwith launched into a verbal tirade against some of his men and the USMC pilots. He shouted at his men for leaving their weapons on board the burning C-130, the stress and frustration of this operation was now pouring out in understandable emotional outbursts. He accused the pilots of being cowards and at this point it was clear that he really hadn't appreciated what they had been through. One of his senior NCOs politely informed him that these soldiers were lucky to be alive, and clearly at the time of the aircraft and helicopter collision they had other things on their minds rather than their weapons; their main concern being their lives and the lives of their colleagues. Colonel Beckwith apologized for the outburst, knowing that no matter what happened, he would be blamed. All in all, he was the man on the ground and everyone else would fade into the background leaving him responsible. The senior staff who debriefed him were surprisingly understanding about the mission's failures, and clearly felt that it was sheer bad luck that this operation had failed, rather then poor planning.

When Colonel Beckwith returned to the states, the President informed him that he would like to visit Delta to thank them for what they had done in Iran. President Carter personally shook the hand of every Delta Operator that had been involved in the mission, and put his arm around Colonel Beckwith to reassure him that he wasn't to blame for the failure of the operation and that, ultimately as President, he took the blame. Had this operation succeeded President Carter would have been America's hero and would have been re-elected in the forthcoming election. Failure, however, has few friends and the election was won by Ronald Reagan, with Jimmy Carter pushed into the political shadows.

Colonel Beckwith had his own problems to face. The military wanted him to face a press conference to answer questions on Operation 'Eagle Claw'. Colonel Beckwith had dealt with the press in Vietnam and had no problems with them. However this time he tried desperately to avoid attending the conference, his reason being Delta. Delta at this time was still secret and he wanted to make sure it stayed that way. Colonel Beckwith faced the might of the American Press and coped well with the questions, parrying away the most awkward ones that hinted at Delta and its existence. On one occasion during the press conference he was asked the question, "Colonel, you said you had never rehearsed aborting the mission?" The Colonel replied, "With a 130 on fire and all that – no, we'd not done that, Sir." It was a good answer and proved that in the eyes of the American public, he was an honourable soldier who had tried very hard to pull off a daring mission to rescue American citizens and it had gone tragically wrong. The blame however was not his, or his Delta team, or even the USMC pilots, it was simply bad luck, nothing more, nothing less.

There were those who suggested that the failure in the Desert was a blessing in disguise, due to the fact that had they entered Teheran and had a shoot out with the Iranians, there would have been major political problems with the Soviet Union and the Arab world. In the end the hostages were released unharmed eight months later, however twenty years later, the debate still goes with regards what should have been done. The Americans in the year 2001 are claiming compensation from the Iranians for the loss of their embassy and some fifty books have been published addressing the crisis. Yet even today many questions remain unanswered.

In military terms Operation 'Eagle Claw' failed to achieve its objective. However, the modern American Special Forces and their sophisticated capabilities owe much to 'Eagle Claw' and Delta. For a period after 'Eagle Claw', America enjoyed a relatively calm political stage and it can be argued that a very powerful message was sent out to the world – that if anyone harms US citizens or military personnel then they will be pursued.

With regards to the pilots in Operation 'Eagle Claw', it is doubtful if any other service could have done better then the USMC crews that took part. The arguments will always rage that the USAF should have been given the mission. This in part is understandable, as they are equipped and experienced to fly longer missions, and they did carry out the Son Tay raid. But far from being cowards the USMC crews that flew the mission were good pilots, who were given a task well beyond the capabilities of man and machine and gave everything. Colonel Seiffert the USMC commander summed up the problem 'Aircraft broke, plain and simple.'

The Halloway Special Operations Review Group carried out a study, and reported twenty three different factors that contributed to the failure of the mission. The weather teams were criticized along with the standards of maintenance performed by the Navy before the operation took place. The wrong air filters were used on the engine intakes, together with the wrong grading of lubricants; this caused heating problems as well as performance degradation flying in the hot desert environment. The USMC pilots seemed to have been in a no-win situation and little did they know that on the afternoon of 24 April, as they climbed aboard their RH-53D Sea Stallion helicopters, that they were all boarding the 'Chariots of the Damned.'

CHAPTER 4
THE NIGHT STALKERS
Mike Ryan

More than any other operational failure that had occurred before 1980, Operation 'Rice Bowl' focused America's military thinking. In particular Delta force, who played such a major role in the Iran hostage crisis, vowed that, for helicopter support during an operation, they would never be dependent on any other service again. Their bitter experience with the USMC pilots flying Navy Sea Stallions during 'Eagle Claw' had made them determined to form an Army Special Forces helicopter unit, that would be able to support them in any future military operations.

As a result of Delta's experience in Iran, the United States Army began to develop a special operations aviation capability. Initially, volunteers with above average flying skills were selected from the 101st Aviation groups C/158 and D/158 (UH-60), A/159th (CH-47), and B/229th (OH-6) units to form 'Task Force 158.' They would have the ability to carry out short, medium and long range operations with its own fleet of helicopters, without support from the other services. They would develop their own tactics, combat procedures, and concept of operations that were relevant to Special Forces' mission profiles. The 101st had been selected for this role for a number of reasons. They were the first unit to field the UH-60 Black Hawk helicopter, which was a quantum leap forward compared to the much loved UH-1. The Black Hawk had better range capabilities then any other comparable helicopter and had proven to be extremely reliable in service – with these qualities it was a perfect helicopter for demanding Special Forces operations. In addition to the Black Hawk, the 101st also operated a large number of medium-lift CH-47 Chinook helicopters, along with the small highly agile OH-6 helicopters. In June 1980, Task Force 158 commenced intensive flight training at night, at very low level, using night vision goggles. Their operational doctrine was to operate at night in very close formations, so it was imperative that they train in demanding and realistic conditions to simulate operational missions.

After 'Eagle Claw', the Army recognized that to train pilots for highly demanding Special Forces operations required a great deal of time. In many cases there would not be enough time to develop such skills at short notice, therefore it was imperative to have a standing capability available at a moments notice to deploy anywhere in the world. So, the decision was taken to form a standing Army Aviation Special Operations Task Force to be known as Task Force 160. This was made up of volunteers from Task Force 158, and quickly established a good reputation for always being in the right place at the right time with the right assets.

On 1 April 1982, Task Force 160 was designated as the 160th Aviation Battalion (although they are however still referred to as Task Force 160). What the 160th needed now was a mission, and in October 1983 they got one. On 21 October 1983, the unit received notice that it was to deploy to Barbados, for combat operations in Grenada as part of Operation 'Urgent Fury'. Operation 'Urgent Fury' had been hastily put together in response to events that had taken place on the Caribbean Island of Grenada on 19 October 1983. Grenadian Prime Minister, Maurice Bishop, and a number of his aides had been executed by the People's Revolutionary Army (PRA), on the orders of a new radical political group known as the 'Revolutionary Military Council' (RMC). This act had aroused America's interest for several reasons. Maurice Bishop had been sympathetic to Marxist ideology and had come to power as a result of a coup in 1979. He had been friendly with Fidel Castro of Cuba, and the Americans feared that another Cuban satellite state was about to be developed in their back yard. Reports of a Soviet military build-up on Grenada had started to concern America, due to the fact that large numbers of new buildings and a 10,000ft runway had just been constructed on the site of Point Salines International Airport. Grenada claimed that this was for tourism, however the United States Government believed otherwise. After the Cuban Missile crisis of the sixties, America was paranoid about Castro and Cuba. President Ronald Reagan was determined to ensure that Cuba never got a foothold in Grenada and this act of violence was just the excuse that he needed to order American Forces in. President Reagan faced a problem, in world terms he simply couldn't send American Forces into Grenada without a major justification. He was made aware of the fact that 1,000 American medical students were on the Island, and if an impression could be created that their lives were at risk, a military response could be justified.

America as a nation had been desperate to restore its prestige after a series of military disasters, including Operation 'Eagle Claw'. American foreign policy had vowed that never again would its citizens be taken hostage long-term, and that if such a situation ever occurred again, America would take strong action at the first sight of trouble. The Pentagon rumour machine was in overdrive at this time, stories about Grenada were being blown out of all proportion, and to the American public they were looking at another Cuba Crisis in the making. The new regime that had taken power in Grenada were even more extreme than Bishop's Marxist government before, and the new leader General Hudson Austin and his sixteen member RMC quickly took control of the Island. Grenada had hundreds of American citizens residing there and President Reagan felt that they might be in danger from the new government and its followers.

President Reagan decided that he must act and authorized a non-combatant evacuation operation (NEO). This had two purposes, one to protect American Citizens, the other to restore a more mainstream government to Grenada. Before commencing the operation he needed to have a legal justification for invading an independent neighbour that was part of the commonwealth, especially as its British Governor-General, Sir Paul Scoon, acted on behalf of the British head of state, Queen Elizabeth. What America needed was a request from the Governor-General to invade Grenada and restore law and order, but how would they obtain that? They presumed that the governor-general had been taken prisoner by the new government and would have written a letter requesting intervention from outside.

America decided that Sir Paul Scoon was being held in Richmond Hill Prison, against his will, and must be rescued at once. President Ronald Reagan ordered the invasion of Grenada and the operation was to be known as 'Urgent Fury'. It was to be spearheaded by the US Navy SEALs, who would insert a small team into Grenada by parachuting them into the sea with their own boats. Then, under cover of the night they would take up positions near Point Salines Airport and report back to the command and control centre with any intelligence gained.

The SEALs had been chosen for this operation due to the fact that they had carried out an exercise simulating incursions into Grenada only a year before. They had planned the exercise just like a real operation and had prepared survey sites, along with methods of insertion – clearly making them the right people for the job. In their original plan, the insertion method was to be by destroyer, which was to sail near to Grenada and remain out of sight over the horizon. The destroyer would then send ashore small inflatables via a small island known as Glover Island, which was off the coast of Point Salines.

The plan had been well thought out by the SEALs, due to the considerable amount of intelligence data obtained during their training exercise on this part of the island. On 21 October, President Reagan gave the order to invade Grenada. The SEALs were to be the first in, and an insertion was planned for 23 October. This accelerated decision meant that they would not be able to operate with their original plan, and a totally different method of insertion would have to be used. They looked at the idea of using helicopters, however they were unable to carry the SEALs' inflatables due to the high winds over the open sea; so another method would have to be used. The mission planners decided on an at-sea rendezvous, by paradrop, with a link up to a destroyer. The mission began with a delay that was to have disastrous consequences for the SEAL team. Two C-130 transporters took off late, with the SEAL teams and inflatables aboard. They each carried an eight-man team along with an inflatable monohull boat.

They arrived over the open ocean drop zone just before dusk instead of in the afternoon. The winds were now well above acceptable safety limits and the operation should have been cancelled. The jump commenced, however a parachute release mechanism on the inflatable boat failed and as a result the inflatable overturned and was dragged along by its open parachute. The eight SEALs who had been dropped with the inflatable were now struggling in the water with their heavy kit and ultimately three of them drowned. The other five were picked up by the destroyer, *USS Clifton Sprague*. The operation was now in serious trouble although having only just begun. The second C-130 dropped its SEAL team and inflatable near to what it perceived was the destroyer. However, it was in fact a commercial cargo ship and disaster was about to strike twice. The parachute release worked fine on this occasion, but one of the members of the SEAL team failed to reach the inflatable because of the high seas and drowned. A massive search and rescue operation commenced, but failed to find him alive. As a result of this major setback Operation 'Urgent Fury' was delayed by another day. Even though the SEALs had lost close members of their team, they tried to make a landing, as planned, on Point Salines. However they spotted what they believed to be a Grenadan patrol boat and had to turn back, as they were under strict instructions to avoid any contact with the enemy at this critical phase of the operation.

On 24 October, the entire mission was attempted again, but they had to abort due to the severe winds over the sea – even though they were extremely close to Grenada. On 25 October, the invasion of Grenada en masse occurred, but there were no secret insertions, as they had all failed on the two previous nights. Instead Grenada saw a good old-fashioned invasion carried out in traditional ways, just like in the Pacific and Europe during WW2.

The Marines were planning a massive beach assault using landing craft and small vehicles, but as a result of the high surf around Grenada this was not possible. Instead they deployed by helicopter and in the early hours of 25 October, USMC helicopters moved into the area of Grenville without any significant problems. Several other priority targets were identified for helicopter assaults, among them Fort Rupert and Richmond Hill Prison. It had been decided that the 160th were to carry out a night assault against Richmond Hill Prison as they were the best qualified for such a mission.

The 160th had flown to a staging post in Barbados from their base in Fort Campbell, Kentucky, and were keen to take part in Operation 'Urgent Fury'. This was to be their baptism of fire. Their first mission was to assault the Richmond Hill Prison that overlooked the town of St. Georges. Intelligence reports advised that the prison held Sir Paul Scoon along with other civil servants, who had been arrested by the RMC regime. The Richmond Hill Prison was built on the site of an old fort, which was overlooked by Fort Frederick, a manned garrison used by the People's Revolutionary Army. The plan was simple. Between the two forts was a small valley, nine of the 160th's Black Hawk helicopters were to fly through the valley at low level towards Richmond Hill Prison. As they approached the Prison, they were to move to pre-designated positions around the fort, the helicopters would then flare and go into a hover position, to allow the Special Forces and Rangers to fastrope to the ground for their assault.

As the operation was being planned, an inter-service dispute broke out over timings and methods of insertion causing the mission to be delayed, with disastrous consequences. At 0630 hours the helicopters departed for their mission. With nine Black Hawks and two MH-6 Little Bird helicopters assigned for fire-support – this operation should have been simple. The 160th were very angry about being deployed during daylight hours, as their tactics were designed for night-time operations. As the assault force proceeded towards the prison at low level, they suddenly came under intense gun-fire from two gun positions located on a ridge above the prison. These gun emplacements were equipped with twin 23mm ZSU-23-2 cannons that can prove lethal to helicopters. Intelligence had reported that opposition would be light, and that there were no AAA (Anti-Aircraft Artillery) emplacements in this area.

The helicopters made easy targets as they flew down the valley, silhouetted against the morning sun. The Black Hawks were under intense fire, and could not get near to the prison. The 23mm cannons had been expertly sited to cover any possible landing areas around the prison, in addition there were heavy machine guns mounted on the roof of the prison, making a fastrope assault impossible. The lead helicopter, flown by Captain Keith Lucas, flew into a hail of bullets and both him and his co-pilot were wounded. The other Black Hawks desperately tried to find a place to land, however there were no suitable areas available. Although every helicopter had been hit, all were still flying and they broke off their attack and regrouped over the sea ready for another attempt on the heavily defended prison.

The Black Hawk group called for air-support from the powerful AC-130 gunships that were available, but at this time they were committed to other actions elsewhere on Grenada. The helicopters flew in again and were met by heavy gunfire. As they attempted their run, the helicopter crews opened fire with their guns in an attempt to try and suppress the enemy positions – however they were unsuccessful. Captain Lucas was tragically killed in this attack, and despite valiant efforts by his co-pilot to save the Black Hawk it was too badly damaged to continue flying and plunged out of control into a nearby hillside. On hitting the ground the Black Hawk burst into flames, killing all the occupants apart from the co-pilot and crew chief. The other Black Hawk crews looked on in horror as they witnessed the death of some of their colleagues; this should have been a low risk mission, but it was turning into a nightmare for the 160th. They decided at this point to abort the mission and await air-support, as the ground defences were too strong.

After the 160th had landed at their base, they looked over their helicopters to survey the damage that had been inflicted. They were amazed at what they saw, one Black Hawk had 76 bullet holes in its airframe, it had taken hits in both the main rotor and tail rotor and its wounded pilot had still been able to fly it home. Another helicopter took 47 hits through drive shafts, primary systems, hydraulic pumps and its cockpit area, and was also able to return to base without presenting any significant problems to the pilots. Although the mission had failed to achieve its objective, it showed how determined the 160th had been to prove themselves successful. They earned much respect that day from the Special Forces community, their Black Hawk helicopters' ability to absorb severe battle damage giving a new meaning to the word 'survivability.'

Losing several of their fellow aircrew colleagues in this first action was a high price to pay for the 160th. Although they had already paid a high price in getting their pilots to the standards that they displayed during the attack on Richmond Hill Prison. In training, they had already lost seventeen people in five separate flying accidents during 1983 alone. The 160th took some comfort from the fact that the planning for Operation 'Urgent Fury' had been poorly executed and that the failure to take the prison had been the fault of poor intelligence, rather than their execution of the mission.

During the afternoon of the 25 October, American A-7 Corsair aircraft launched an attack on Fort Frederick to knock out the gun emplacements above Richmond Hill Prison. The attack was a failure. Instead of hitting the fort the bombs hit the island's psychiatric hospital killing twenty-one civilians. Because of this dreadful mistake the 160th were unable to return to the prison for a second attack.

The other objective for the 160th was Fort Rupert, a base known to house some of General Austin's senior advisors. The 160th arrived at Fort Rupert with members of the Special Forces who had been assigned the task of assaulting the complex and capturing any of General Austin's forces. The soldiers stormed the Fort and quickly rounded up all of those inside who were loyal to Austin. The operation was a complete success and the 160th were called in to extract both the operators and the detainees to the USS Guam for questioning and processing. The operation had gone very smoothly and there were no casualties or helicopter losses.

Elsewhere on the Island of Grenada, the PRA and its Cuban backers were putting up stiff resistance to the American invasion. The key area of the operation was the assault on Point Salines Airport, which had to be secured to allow reinforcements to be flown in from the US mainland. Early on the morning of 25 October, an AC-130H of the 16th Special Operations Squadron flew over the Point Salines Airport attracting very heavy AAA fire. The aircraft used its advanced sensors to scan the airport for anti-aircraft weapons and runway objects, this valuable intelligence was radioed back to the tactical planners for operations later in the morning.

The pilot of the AC-130, Major Michael Couvillon had taken a great risk flying this mission above the Airport. He kept his aircraft above 6,000 feet to avoid the ZSU-23 20mm anti-aircraft cannons that were located below him. As he orbited the airport he spotted four air-defence sites that could cause significant problems to the transport MC-130 aircraft as they approached. The AC-130 spotted heavy equipment and concrete posts on the runway that would make it impossible to land on. Thanks to the crew's bravery many lives were saved, as had the aircraft tried to land on the runway they would have been shot to pieces. There was too much AAA for a helicopter assault, so the planners decided to make a paradrop instead, using the Rangers. Before this could happen the AAA sites would have to be destroyed. The AC-130 was tasked with knocking out the AAA sites and this it did with great effectiveness, even though its aiming computer was intermittently malfunctioning.

As the Rangers approached Point Salines Airport they were told of the change in plan in mid-air. Instead of landing on the runway, they were to parachute in. This caused a slight problem as none of them were wearing parachutes and they would have to rig up. A normal drop like this should have taken five minutes, but with the delay in donning parachutes this one took over an hour-and-a-half to complete. The aircraft flew over the sea at an altitude of 100 feet. As they approached Point Salines Airport they climbed to 500 feet and the troops jumped. Two Rangers were killed in the jump because of parachute failures – the rest landed and were in action virtually straight away against the Cubans and Grenadans. A couple of machine guns pinned the Rangers down, but these were soon neutralized by the AC-130s above. There were over 650 Cubans and Grenadan troops either on, or near the Airport, and the time taken to clear them away was grossly underestimated. At one stage of the invasion the Americans occupied one side of the Airport, the enemy the other.

Aircraft were now having problems landing, the runway having only been partially cleared, so only one aircraft at a time could land. As a result there was a considerable number of aircraft 'stacked up' waiting to land and this caused serious problems with providing reinforcements. On the ground, some of the Ranger and Airborne units were struggling to make any progress, due to the lack of information on the terrain. Many units had landed without maps, and were highly embarrassed to have to ask locals for directions. In one incident a Ranger showed a local Grenadan his map, stating that he couldn't match the features to the ground; he was politely informed that the map he was holding was of Barbados and not Grenada.

Before the invasion SR-71 Blackbird and TR-1 reconnaissance aircraft were flying regular intelligence gathering missions over Grenada on behalf of the Defence Intelligence Agency. This data was collated and passed over to JSOC, who refused to share it with any of the units participating in Operation 'Urgent Fury'. This was clearly a ridiculous state of affairs, and caused unnecessary problems that could have been avoided.

The main vehicle of transport during the Grenada invasion was the helicopter. Several different types were employed including CH-46s, CH-53 Sea Stallions, Black Hawks, MH-6 'Little Birds' and for fire-support USMC Cobra gunships. October 25th was to be the key day in the invasion, with several large helicopter assaults taking place at various strategic points around the island. North of the capital Saint Georges, Marines landed in force at Grand Mal Bay by both helicopter and landing craft. The island had been divided into two halves for the purpose of planning. The Marines were to seize and hold the northern part of Grenada with the Army taking the south, just like they had done in Okinawa in World War Two. The Marines made up twenty percent of the invasion force, yet they were occupying eighty percent of the island. At Grand Mal Bay, the Marines landed by ship, with a second company flying over from Pearls airfield to reinforce them. The Army and Marines both used UHF radios, however they operated on different frequencies so communication between them was extremely difficult, this was to cause problems throughout the operation.

Over on the other side of the island at Pearls airfield, there were also problems. A shortage of helicopters meant that the lift for the Marines was delayed for several hours. Another problem was the lack of information regarding the Marines mission – nobody had briefed them regarding the assault on Saint Georges, so a meeting had to be arranged on the beach at Grand Mal Bay. This was bad enough, but another problem awaited them, the beach could only handle one helicopter at a time, so they had to jump into the sea and wade ashore. Once briefed, the Marines advanced on Saint Georges without any significant problems.

Earlier in the day they had witnessed the 160th with Delta Force, fly over them on their way to Richmond Hill Prison, some five hours later than they had expected. Some of them observed the fierce fighting that took place during the assault, and were shocked at the level of opposition. Although as the Marines entered Saint Georges they encountered little opposition, their main task now was to link up with the SEALs who had been dropped in earlier in the day. The SEALs mission had been to secure the residence of the Governor-General, Sir Paul Scoon. However they got a shock. As they assaulted the building they found Sir Paul and his wife having tea in one of the rooms within the residence. There were no guards within the compound, and at no point had Sir Paul Scoon been threatened or taken hostage by the Cubans or Grenadans.

The SEALs had been ordered to take Sir Paul Scoon off the island, because of the fear of him being captured by the PRA. It was imperative for the US to justify Operation 'Urgent Fury', so Sir Paul Scoon's endorsement was of the utmost importance to President Reagan. The view of the Operation in the UK was of anger and dismay, especially from the Queen and Prime Minister Margaret Thatcher. The UK felt that the situation in Grenada was unstable rather then dangerous, and if Sir Paul Scoon felt threatened he could have summoned British military assistance at any time. In short the British felt that this was not America's problem. The British had just fought the Falklands War the year before Operation 'Urgent Fury', and had a sizeable military force nearby, so they could have intervened at any time if requested. This situation clearly didn't help America right now. During the assault on the Governor-General's residence the SEAL commander requested urgent assistance, stating that he had been surrounded by Cubans and that eight of his men had been wounded in a fight. This turned out to be a lie that was to have very tragic consequences for the Marines. In reality, the SEALs had run out of ammunition defending the residence and were too embarrassed to admit this.

The Marines over at Pearls airfield immediately despatched two Cobra helicopter gunships for support, however as they flew towards Fort Frederick they were both shot down with the loss of three lives. This was a bitter blow, particularly as these pilots had been in action throughout the day providing valuable support to the ground forces, and were the only casualties that the Marines had during the whole of Operation 'Urgent Fury'.

The eastern side of Grenada had seen action during the day around the Pearls airfield area, where the Marines had landed earlier that morning by helicopter. The landing sites near the airfield were very marshy and as the giant CH-53 transport helicopters landed they began to sink into the soft ground, making unloading very difficult. On one occasion a jeep leaving a helicopter overturned, although fortunately nobody was hurt in this incident. The Marines came under fire from AAA systems that were based at Pearls airfield, however they were quickly silenced by the Marines Cobra gunships. Throughout the day they came under sniper fire which was ineffective and thankfully there were no casualties. The main assault had only taken thirty minutes to accomplish, and compared to the progress of the Army in the South this was extremely fast. At nearby Grenville where Marines had also landed, there was no opposition from the Cubans, and not a single shot was fired throughout the assault.

On 26 October, American forces consolidated their hold on Grenada, and began mopping up the remaining Cuban and Grenadan forces. A massive attack was mounted against Saint Georges and Point Salines airfield to finally secure them, due to the fact that after the first days action around the airfield, the barracks next to the airfield still remained in Cuban hands.

Intelligence had reported medical students in the True Blue campus, which was near the eastern end of the runway. Rangers and airborne forces eventually reached them and ferried them away from Point Salines. During the debriefing of the students it emerged that others were living near to the airfield at Grand Anse campus some four miles North- East of the airfield. Air-reconnaissance had reported that the enemy had dug a defensive line in front of the campus, which backed on to the beach. The strength of the enemy forces was unknown and a two pronged assault was planned against Grand Anse campus. The first assault would be from ground forces via Point Salines airfield, involving Rangers and airborne troops. The second assault would be from the air by Marines using CH-46 Sea Knight helicopters. Before the attack commenced an air strike was called in on the enemy positions, this was carried out by A-7 Corsairs operating from the USS Independence. The air attacks levelled virtually all the buildings near to the campus, and once this was finished the assaults began. Small arms fire was directed towards the Sea Knight helicopters as they transported Rangers towards the campus. One was severely damaged and crash-landed on Grand Anse beach, another was shot down over the sea just off Grand Anse. At the time, some commanders were adamant that the Marine helicopters were shot down by friendly forces and not members of the PRC. This statement was made due to the fact that throughout Operation 'Urgent Fury' there had been unexpected contacts with other forces in areas that were deemed free-fire zones. On one occasion, during the evacuation from the campus, a medical student was seen kissing the ground. A soldier asked him if he was thanking God for being saved from the PRC, he said "No, I'm thanking God that none of you trigger happy 'Son O Bitches' killed us during your attack". He was referring to the fact that none of the medical students had been threatened or taken hostage by the PRC throughout the invasion, and in effect they should have been left alone.

During the assault on Saint Georges, Marines had gone into the Governor-General's residence and relieved the SEALs of their responsibility for Sir Paul Scoon; they took him off the island by helicopter to a nearby US Warship. An air strike on Saint Georges had driven the remaining enemy forces out of the town, so when the Marines stormed Forts Frederick, Lucas, Adolphus and Richmond Hill prison there was no opposition.

The last major action of Operation 'Urgent Fury' occurred at Calvigny Barracks in the South-East of Grenada. Intelligence had reported that the Barracks housed some 600 Cuban soldiers as well as Russian Spetsnaz advisors. Due to the increased threat, A-7 Corsairs and Cobra helicopter gunships were sent in to attack the barracks and neutralize any AAA systems in advance of the helicopter assault. In addition to the air-strikes, US warships and ground based artillery provided fire-support to the assault force. After the bombardment, a Cobra gunship flew over the severely damaged Barracks and confirmed that there was no sign of life. Three Black Hawk helicopters carrying Ranger assault troops flew towards the Barracks and started to come under intermittent rifle fire. The shots were being fired from a distance and were for the most part ineffective. The helicopters felt that the threat was light and continued to move into a landing position. The first Black Hawk flared and landed on the Calvigny Barracks compound. As the Rangers disembarked from the helicopter to take up a defensive position around the barracks, the other two Black Hawks approached to take up a landing position. However when the two helicopters flew in, disaster struck. One of the Black Hawks collided with the other causing it to fall onto the Rangers below. Four Rangers were killed and a number severely injured by the still moving blades. The other Black Hawk crashed nearby, however the injuries to the occupants were minor. This accident was a great tragedy for everybody involved in the Calvigny assault, especially as the Barracks had been evacuated before the Rangers arrived. There were no casualties as a result of enemy action, and the Calvigny assault marked the effective end of Operation 'Urgent Fury'.

The operation had been costly in terms of losses, both in personnel and equipment. American casualties were 29 killed, with 152 injured, while 110 Grenadan and 71 Cuban soldiers were killed. The civilian casualties were extremely high with 45 killed and 358 injured. These figures are very high considering that the operation only lasted three days. America admitted to losing eight helicopters in the operation, however other members of the military believe that the losses were much higher. Many people in the United States felt that on the whole, Operation 'Urgent Fury' was a disaster for America, and should never have happened. The mistakes from the failed Operation 'Eagle Claw' had not been taken into account, even after three years of review. The political fall-out continued for many years after the Grenada action, however many military lessons were learnt that would put America's armed forces in good stead for future conflicts.

After the end of Operation 'Urgent Fury' the 160th evaluated their performance during the conflict and looked at ways in which they could improve their capabilities. They had come out of the conflict with a good reputation as a highly skilled unit, which had much to offer the US armed forces. The conflict also gave them a nickname: 'The Night Stalkers'.

From 1983 to 1986, the 160th continued to hone their skills through constant training and deployments on classified exercises and operations. The 160th had begun its life as an ad hoc unit that needed refining and direction. As a result, the 160th implemented changes that could define their role and place it within America's Order of Battle (ORBAT). Conventional unit criteria was originally applied to the 160th's structure, however it was rather unsuitable as the unit's operational requirements were growing faster than the system's ability to respond; so the unit soon found itself incompatible with normal Special Operations doctrine.

Before the 160th were involved in Operation 'Urgent Fury' they had to deal with a major challenge that greatly affected the unit. From March through to October 1983, the Battalion lost a number of helicopters in a series of accidents that occurred at night. In all, seventeen members of the unit were killed in these accidents and clearly these attrition figures were unacceptable to the Army. A panel was set up to review the 160th, with regard to its structure and method of operation. They made two main recommendations, which eventually led to the formation of a Special Operations Aviation Training Company and the formation of the Systems Integration Maintenance Office.

After the 160th Aviation Battalion's performance in Grenada, it was recognised that the unit needed additional aviation resources, including helicopters. To help meet the increasing demands for support, the 129th Combat Aviation Company was activated on 1 October at Hunter AAF, Georgia. This unit was placed under the command and control of the 160th. The 245th Aviation Battalion from the Oklahoma National Guard was also assigned to support the 160th, with its 25AH-1 and 23 UH-1 helicopters. The 160th Aviation Battalion was reorganized and redesignated as the 160th Aviation Group (Airborne) on 16 October 1986. The new designation of the 160th meant that it had now become an airborne unit, and had the authority to wear the Maroon beret. The unit initially wore the airborne flash and background trimming of 1st SOCOM. The 160th went on to design its own flash and background trimming, that combined both aviation and 1st SOCOM colours. On the 26 March 1987, the Institute of Heraldry, US Army, approved the distinctive flash and background trimming for the 160th.

The formation of the 160th SOAG (A) in October 1986, was an interim step in the creation of one special operations aviation unit to serve as a unifying headquarters for all Army Special Operations Aviation. By 1987, plans were underway to create a

SOF Aviation Brigade at Hunter AAF. In addition, Training & Doctrine Command (TRADOC) was tasked to submit a layout of the design concept plan for the 160th Aviation Group.

During August 1987, the US Army Aviation Centre at Fort Rucker proposed that the 160th SOAG be regimentally designated as separate companies and one Battalion of the 7th Aviation Regiment. In October and November 1987, the 160th and 1st SOCOM requested that the 160th SOAG (A) be redesignated as the 160th Aviation Regiment, instead of the 7th Aviation Regiment. Although the 160th was a relatively new unit, it had been combat tested, earned two citations, and had a special operations affiliation. The activation of the 160th Aviation Regiment was approved under the US Army Regimental System.

In 1988 a report by the CG 1st SOCOM identified a number of problems within the 160th that related to over commitment and an inadequate force structure. In June 1988, 1st SOCOM prepared a concept brief on the formation of a Special Operations Aviation Regiment (SOAR) and briefed the Commander in Chief, US Special Operations Command. After receiving Army and TRADOC concurrence, the 160th SOAG (A) was redesignated as the 160th Special Operations Aviation Regiment (Airborne) with an effective date of May 16th, 1990. A Regimental activation ceremony was held on June 28th 1990.

During the Eighties, the 160th found themselves involved in a number of Military operations that helped further their skills and reputation. Operation ' Urgent Fury' in 1983 had given the 'Night Stalkers' their baptism of fire. They had learned a lot from the Grenada mission, their experience there helping to refine tactics and methods of operation – giving the 160th a well deserved reputation for getting the job done. In 1987, the 160th were sent to the Persian Gulf to participate in Operation 'Prime Chance'. This operation was initiated to protect ships passing through the Persian Gulf, who were being attacked by Iranians using small power boats fitted with heavy calibre machine guns. In addition to these harassments on international shipping, the Iranians were also laying mines in the paths of ships in an attempt to sink them.

This situation could no longer be tolerated, and the United States took decisive and robust action against the Iranians. The Night Stalkers supported a joint military task force in very difficult and demanding conditions. The Iranians tended to lay their mines at night, which was done to avoid detection from helicopters and warships patrolling the area.

The Iranians however were unaware that the Night Stalkers operated at night as a matter of routine and were able to beat them at their own game. Aircrews of the 160th operated 30 feet above the water at night, using night-vision goggles in an attempt to deter the Iranians. Their patience eventually paid off. Operation 'Prime Chance' saw the first engagement at night using aviator night-vision goggles and FLIR (Forward Looking Infrared) systems. The Night Stalkers were successful in their engagement, and their presence in the Persian Gulf deterred further enemy attacks on international shipping and slowed the mine-laying process.

Around the same time as Operation 'Prime Chance', the 160th received notice that they were to take part in another operation. This mission was to fly into a remote location in Africa and recover a Soviet-built Mi-24 Hind attack helicopter. In June 1988, two MH-47 helicopters deployed to Africa for the recovery operation, known as 'Mount Hope III'. The crews took off at night for this mission and were required to fly 490 miles without outside navigational aids. The MH-47 crews were forced to battle their way through a blinding sandstorm to reach the Hind. They arrived at their destination and recovered the helicopter and brought it back for evaluation. This mission again proved that the 160th were a highly capable unit, well enough equipped to undertake many different types of mission profiles. In December 1989, the 160th found themselves on standby, yet again, for another mission. This time they were going to be operating closer to home in Panama, Central America.

The background to this operation can be traced back to the late 1980's, when Panama's leader, General Manuel Noriega, was indicted in an American Court for drug offences. Noriega had been a major irritant to the United States for many years, as he was seen as a major league drug trafficker for the South American drug cartels. On December 15th 1989, Noriega survived a failed coup d'etat, and went on Panamanian TV to declare war on the United States. Tension between the two countries was now high, and America clearly felt that something had to give. On 16 December an incident occurred that pushed America over the edge. A USMC Lieutenant was murdered by Panamanian soldiers at a roadblock, allegedly for failing to stop for them. This was the final straw for America and an Operation known as 'Just Cause' was activated on Wednesday 20th December 1989. In the early hours of the morning, US Navy SEALs attacked Paitilla Airport, where it was believed Noriega kept a Learjet. AC-130H Spectre gunships of the 16th Special Operations Squadron identified key targets around Panama City, including the Panama Defence Forces Fortress known as the La Commandancia.

Another key target hit was the Puma Battalion barracks outside Omar Torrijos Airport. The initial assault on Panama was massive with over 7000 American troops inserted on the first day alone, and the operation would eventually see the deployment of some 22,500 US personnel. The first wave of the assault involved 77 C-141B Starlifters, 22 C-130 Hercules and 12 C-5 Galaxies. The assault was divided into five groups and a total of 84 airdrops took place. After the first wave was deployed, a second wave of 40 C-141s and 13 C-5s followed in. It was a huge operation that involved many aircraft and helicopters. The first operational deployment of the F-117A Nighthawk also took place during 'Just Cause'. Flying non-stop from Nevada, with the support of air refuelling, the USAF sent two Nighthawks from the 37th TFW down to support the operation. They dropped 2,000-lb LGBs in a field near to a Panamanian barracks to scare the troops into surrendering.

On the ground the160th were tasked with several key missions to ensure the liberation of Panama. At the time of their order to move they had been training at Fort Campbell in cold winter conditions – in Panama the contrast couldn't have been more different. At that time of the year the temperatures in Panama were into the high nineties every day with very high humidity factors, making conditions for man and machine very difficult. The 160th deployed to Panama in strength; they had some 450 personnel available, along with 9 MH-6, 11 AH-6G/J, 19 UH/MH-60A, and 7 MH-47Ds. The 160th sent most of their helicopters into Panama by transport aircraft. However, three MH-47Ds self-deployed from Fort Campbell to Howard AFB in Panama, via Hurlburt Field in Florida, where they linked up with USAF MH-53s from the 1st SOW.

The 160th were involved in the first pre H-Hour airborne and air assaults, along with the Rangers and 82nd Airborne who parachuted into Torrijos Airport and the Puma barracks. A second Ranger battalion parachuted into Rio Hato where some of Noriega's most feared soldiers were based. The key to the success of Operation 'Just Cause' lay in the seizure of three airfields. The US feared that Noriega would use his Learjet to escape the American invasion by flying to another South American country where no extradition treaty with the US existed. It was therefore imperative to cut-off any possible escape routes as rapidly as possible. The three airfields were Tocumen Military Airfield, Omar Torrijos International Airport, and Rio Hato Military Airfield. The assaults on the airfields were carried out using C-130s and C-141s escorted by AC-130 Spectre gunships along with AH-6 Little Bird helicopters. The 75th Ranger Regiment carried out the assaults, with little opposition from the Panamanians. They killed seven of Noriega's troops without any losses, and only one Ranger was seriously injured.

The main helicopter operations were carried out by the USAF MH-53Js and Army Black Hawks. Within Panama City, Noriega had a number of bases, which were heavily fortified. The 160th had the perfect helicopter for urban warfare, the AH-6 Little Bird. The AH-6 with its small size and nimble performance was able to weave in and out of the narrow streets of Panama City with ease. Its armament of mini-guns and rockets were perfect for close quarter combat and in the highly skilled hands of the 160th, these helicopters were a tremendous asset to the invasion force.

One of the main targets in Panama City was the PDF headquarters known as La Commandancia. This was a major fortress surrounded by high rise apartments that were occupied by Panamanian snipers. On December 20th, American conventional forces launched an assault on La Commandancia supported by air-cover from the 160th using their AH-6 Little Birds. In all, the

160th allocated four AH-6s to this operation, their main purpose being to scout ahead of the ground troops and engage any PDF troops that presented a threat. As the AH-6s advanced towards La Commandancia they started to come under effective enemy fire. One of the lead helicopters flown by Chief Warrant Officer (CWO) Fred Horsley and Captain George Kunkel, was hit several times as it crested a hill near to La Commandancia. The Little Bird had been flying a low-level, nap-of-the-earth mission profile, with the crew using night-vision goggles. Their mission was to suppress enemy sniper and heavy machine gun fire emanating from a sixteen-storey high-rise apartment that overlooked La Commandancia. Horsley and Kunkel were well aware of the fact that their helicopter had taken a number of direct hits, however all the systems onboard seemed to be functioning well, so they made a decision to remain where they were and carry on with their mission.

Horsley and Kunkel initiated their first attack run against PDF snipers that were operating from the roof of the apartment building, using the helicopters main weapon – its mini-gun. As they completed their attack, they suddenly found that the controls of their helicopter had locked, and it was proving to be increasingly difficult to keep it in the air. Both crew members fought to get the controls of the helicopter to respond, however it was futile. They did their best to steer towards an open area that ran alongside a building and managed to level the Little Bird before it hit the ground. The helicopter skidded across a courtyard and crashed into a concrete post. As the crew struggled to get out, the helicopter caught fire trapping Kunkel inside. Fortunately he was able to free himself and escaped out of Horsley's side. They were however in the Devil's mouth, the Little Bird had landed in La Commandancia itself, and the PDF were shooting at them with everything that they had. The pilots faced another problem, above them an AC-130 Spectre gunship was directing its fire against the compound where they were stranded. They seemed to be facing two possible fates: to die from friendly fire or from enemy fire.

Just as they were trying to figure out how to escape from their desperate plight, the firing above them ceased and a massive fire-fight commenced outside the building between the PDF and Task Force Gator, the US 5th Infantry Division. Horsley and Kunkel decided to take advantage of the attack, and escape. As they moved towards the outer wall, which was topped by barbed wire, a PDF soldier approached them with his hands in the air. Horsley drew his pistol and took the Panamanian prisoner, he explained that most of his colleagues had either been killed or had run away, hence his surrender. Kunkel decided that he would climb over the wall and contact Task Force Gator as his night-vision goggles were still working. As Kunkel made his way down the nearby street, he shouted the word 'Bulldog' – this was the recognized password for US Forces in Panama. He quickly made contact with elements of the Task Force, who escorted him back to La Commandancia to recover Horsley and the Panamanian Prisoner. They were then taken back to a high school, from where they were evacuated back to their unit.

Elsewhere in Panama, the 160th were heavily committed to supporting the invasion. During the pre H-Hour insertion, two MH-6s supported by two AH-6s inserted a Combat Control team along with a homing beacon into Torrijos-Tocumen Airport. In addition, four AH-6s with a FARP (Forward Arming and Refuelling Point) MH-60 provided fire support for the airborne assault at Rio Hato. The Army also sent in two AH-64 Apache gunships for heavy fire support. These Apaches were from the 82nd Division, and were OPCON to the 160th. Originally nine other MH-60s and four MH-6s were assigned to assault a key PDF stronghold located near to Rio Hato. However several hours before H-Hour some of Noriega's key personnel were believed to be in a beach house near to Colon, so this Force was redirected there.

As Operation 'Just Cause' got into full swing another key target was identified that had to be given top priority – the Pacora River Bridge. This bridge was of great importance as it stood between Fort Cimmaron and Torrijos Airport and was a good spot for mounting an ambush, as it performed as a natural choke point. The 3rd Battalion, 7th Special Forces Group, designated as Task Force (TF) Black, were tasked with tracking down Noriega and disrupting his command and control networks. The capture of Noriega was given top priority, as his demise would lead to the collapse of PDF resistance. Colonel Jake Jacobelly, the commander of the 7th group, identified three targets for surveillance and four targets for seizure. The targets to be seized were the Pacora River Bridge, Tinajitas, Fort Cimmaron, and a television tower that was to be used for American Psychological Operations (Psyops). Tinajitas housed a PDF garrison that could either target American Forces at Fort Clayton or be used for deploying additional troops to La Commandancia.

Fort Cimmaron also presented a serious threat, as it was the garrison of Battalion 2000, the elite military unit that had come to Noriega's rescue during the Giroldi coup in 1989. The Special Forces planned to launch a direct assault on Cimmaron, either to take their surrender or defeat them if necessary.

The 160th were assigned the task of flying the Special Forces to the Pacora River Bridge. As they prepared to leave their base in Albrook Air Station they started to come under enemy fire.

This attack wasn't expected and threw the timetable of their mission out. An urgent message from Intelligence, advised that a PDF convoy was moving towards the Pacora River Bridge. Major Kevin Higgins, the commander of A Company, and his 24 soldiers decided to move out immediately towards the bridge. As the three MH-60 Black Hawk helicopters lifted into the air with their Special Forces Operators, they were fired on from outside the airfield perimeter. None of the helicopters sustained any damage. The Black Hawks lost no time in attempting to avoid the fire-fight; being shot at went with the territory. Their mission was simple: prevent Battalion 2000 reinforcing the PDF at Torrijos International Airport. Within minutes of leaving their base the 160th and their passengers were on scene at the Pacora River Bridge. As the Black Hawks flew over the bridge, they could see the enemy convoy below them – the first vehicle was on the bridge as they landed nearby.

There was no time wasted by the Special Forces team, as soon as they got to the bridge they opened fire on the lead vehicle with an anti-tank weapon. Although they hit the vehicle it continued moving towards them. At this point they decided to call in an AC-130 Spectre gunship, As the gunship got into a firing position the soldiers in the convoy began to dismount. The Spectre opened fire on the lead vehicle and destroyed it with a shot from its 105mm Howitzer. The enemy mounted a small attack on the Special Forces team, however it was beaten back. Once the Spectre had finished its mission over the bridge, the Panamanians mounted another attack against the SF team – again it was foiled.

A short time later the SF team were relieved by members of the quick reaction force, manned by members of the 82nd Airborne. During the American forces briefing for Operation

'Just Cause' it had been drummed into the soldiers taking part in the invasion, that they were liberators for the Panamanian people and not their enemies. It was therefore imperative that they tried to obtain the surrender of the PDF, rather than just kill them to make up the body count. In this case Operation 'Just Cause' was very successful. At times the American commanders would telephone the PDF and give them a fire-power demonstration of their equipment, before inviting their surrender. In many cases it was a very successful tactic, with a number of PDF units surrendering without firing a shot.

After the initial assault missions, the 160th moved around Panama providing support to Special Forces units that were engaged in securing outlying areas, and searching for renegade Noriega supporters and their hidden weapon caches. Over the next two weeks the 160th conducted numerous air assaults in support of ground forces. One particular operation conducted around Colon, in the North of Panama, involved four MH-60s, two MH-6s, two AH-6s and two MH-47s. On the opening night of 'Just Cause', the 160th and Delta carried out a rescue operation, code-named 'Acid Gambit'. This mission was carried out against a Panamanian prison where an American citizen was being held captive. This US citizen had lived in Panama for a number of years, and was involved with an underground radio station, the Voice of Liberty. The station had been on the air for over a year broadcasting anti-Noriega messages. Noriega's soldiers soon found the radio station and closed it down. The freedom fighters who ran it were imprisoned in Noriega's infamous Modelo Prison. The leader of the freedom activists, Kurt Muse, was put under direct arrest, with an armed guard next to him. The guard's orders were to kill him, if the Americans ever tried a rescue attempt.

At 1215 hours on 20 December 1989, American Special Forces stormed the Modelo Prison. Within minutes of the assault commencing, SF soldiers blew the door of Muse's cell open and told him that they were there to take him home. Muse was escorted to a nearby Little Bird helicopter that belonged to the 160th. They had only just taken off, when they started to come under effective enemy fire. The Little Bird had been hit numerous times, along with the SF team inside. The helicopter's airframe was badly damaged and the pilots were struggling to keep it in the air, they spotted an open area and aimed for it. As the helicopter hit the ground, a number of the SF team were hurt in the crash, although by incredible luck Muse was unhurt. After a period of time American ground forces with armoured personnel carriers reached the scene and picked up Muse and his rescuers and brought them to safety. Thankfully all of the SF team recovered from their injuries and Kurt Muse went on to thank his rescuers in person for saving his life and giving back his freedom. Although to the 160th and Delta, it was just another job.

As for Noriega, he realized that his position was untenable and fled to the Vatican Embassy, where he sought refuge. Noriega stayed in the Vatican Ambassador's residence, before surrendering to American Special Forces on 3 January1990. After his surrender, resistance collapsed and the 160th were tasked with transporting him from the Papal Nuncio to Howard AFB, where he boarded a waiting MC-130 for transportation back to the United States. Noriega eventually faced a trial, and is now imprisoned in Florida.

The casualties during Operation 'Just Cause' included 23 American and 200 Panamanian combatants, in addition there were 202 Panamanian civilian fatalities. The American aircraft damaged included 11 C-130s, and one OH-58, with three AH-6s shot down. Compared to Operation 'Urgent Fury' in 1983, these casualties were relatively light, and again the 160th had proved their worth under very difficult circumstances.

After their return from Panama in early 1990, the 160th began to catch up on training and maintenance schedules that had been missed due to their deployment on Operation 'Just Cause'. They had barely started back into their unit routine, when on 2 August 1990, they received word that Kuwait had been invaded and occupied by the Iraqi Army. As standard operational procedure, the alert status for the 160th was heightened and at the same time the unit started to make provisional arrangements for deployment.

The initial plans called for the deployment of sixteen MH-47s from the 2nd Battalion, however they only had twelve available. As a result 3rd Battalion was tasked with providing four MH-47s and eight MH-60s to back up the 2nd Battalion. After a series of debates within the 160th regarding exactly what assets they were to deploy, it was agreed that as a final deployment they would provide two MH-47s and eight MH-60s from 3rd Battalion and two MH-47s from 2nd Battalion. They were to be deployed on 3 September1990, to King Khalid International Airport.

This operation was going to be the largest deployment of American forces since the Vietnam War; its name "Desert Storm". At the start of the air war, TF3/160 had two missions. Their first was to provide MH-47s to support the pre-H Hour attack on Iraqi air defence ground control intercept sites; their job was to provide fuel bladder helicopters to refuel the AH-64 Apache attack helicopters from the 101st Airborne Division MSLT. Their second mission was to forward deploy to Rafha, where they were to provide a Combat Search and Rescue

(CSAR) capability. Their role would have been to fly into Iraq, and rescue downed allied pilots, however the need for such a forward-deployed unit was deemed unnecessary because of the low allied aircraft losses. As a result the TF/160 were withdrawn from Rafha and moved back to King Khalid Airport.

The 160th were very successful in the execution of their tasks and two missions in particular were quite outstanding. On one combat mission the 160th, flew sixty miles inside Iraqi territory to rescue a downed F-16 pilot. This mission was of great interest, due to the fact that it was the only rescue of the Gulf War, carried out at night using night-vision goggles. They also carried out a daring emergency extraction of a Special Forces 'A' team that had been compromised. The mission was conducted by a single helicopter, in daylight, and in the middle of a serious firefight. The background to this amazing story can be traced back to February 1991, when the 5th Special Forces Group (Airborne) performed several reconnaissance missions in support of the 3rd US Army. Their mission was to carry out surveillance and intelligence gathering on Iraqi Forces, in some cases this involved insertions into Iraqi territory as deep as 165 miles.

The key reason for these missions was to spot build-ups of enemy forces and equipment in the event that they tried preparing counter attacks against the Coalition Forces. The main threat from Iraq, was their elite Republican Guard and this unit in particular had a number of American SF teams assigned to observe their movements. It was standard operational procedure (SOP) during Operation "Desert Storm", for Special Forces to lay-up near Main Supply Routes (MSR) for surveillance missions. There was however, a down side to this practice. Many Iraqi shepherds and Bedouins, would wander around or near the MSRs, making the risk of detection high.

On 23 February 1991, two SF teams were inserted deep into Iraqi territory for Special Reconnaissance missions. Team SR 008B was a small team, commanded by a Master Sergeant, inserted into the Euphrates river valley the night before the Coalition Forces ground invasion. The SF team was under the operational control of the Airborne Corps, its mission was to report on any Iraqi forces or vehicles moving through its sector. As the team were being inserted into their drop off point (DOP), they suddenly heard the sound of dogs barking close to their location. This alarmed them, as the dogs probably belonged to a Bedouin group. They decided to make a run for it towards their hide point, which was located near to an MSR and railway line. The SF team arrived at the hide point, and quickly dug in, as they had to be under cover by daylight. The hide site was located in a mound of dirt in a cultivated field, near to the intersection of two drainage ditches. As the sun rose, they were well-hidden, and already reporting on road and rail movements.

As the morning developed, local shepherds and their families began working in the fields near to the hide site. They moved around the field chasing goats and camels that they owned, and were rapidly getting closer and closer to the SF team. Throughout "Desert Storm" the lack of adequate cover played a major part in a number of missions being compromised. The most famous, being the discovery of the British SAS team *Bravo Two-Zero*.

By midday it was becoming obvious, that with the number of people strolling around near to the hide site, they were going to be discovered. Sure enough, it had to happen. A little girl and her father had noticed that the mound seemed slightly different to what they were used to seeing, and proceeded to walk up to, and around it. As they did so, they spotted a small exit hole leading from the mound that was too big for an animal to have created. They were just about to peer into the hole, when two members of the SF team made an attempt to snatch them. They grabbed the two, and a struggle began. The soldiers tried to explain that they were not going to hurt them, but it was in vain. Their shouting and screaming had attracted a group of some twenty Bedouins, who were nearby. The SF team realized that they were now fully compromised, and had to make a swift withdrawal.

As they ran, the Bedouins opened fire on them; they had been under the impression that the SF team were allied pilots and if they captured them, they would receive a cash reward from the Iraqi Army. The SF team jumped into one of the drainage ditches and made an attempt to put some distance between themselves and the Bedouins. They paused for a moment, to send out an urgent signal for Tactical Air support (Tac-Air), along with a request for a hot extraction, as this area was going to get very busy, very soon. The team got into a defensive position, as they anticipated an attack at any minute.

They didn't have to wait long. One of the Bedouins had flagged down a convoy of Iraqi soldiers and informed them of what they had seen. The Iraqi soldiers immediately jumped out of their vehicles and began firing in the direction of the American Special Forces team. Some of them climbed onto the roofs of their vehicles, providing covering fire, while the others attempted a flanking manoeuvre. On paper the highly trained American Forces could easily challenge the Iraqi conscript soldiers, however in sheer terms of numbers they outgunned the SF team and had more ammunition. Almost two hours passed when, to the delight of the SF team, an American F-16 appeared overhead. The pilot was responding to the request for air-support, and started to commence an attack run. As he dived towards the fighting on the ground, he was unclear as to where the SF team were located. The team on the ground told him to drop a 1000lb bomb in the middle of the action and they would adjust fire from there. After the F-16 had dropped his bomb, the SF team were able to give precise details of where to drop the next bomb. The F-16 then dropped a cluster bomb on top of the Iraqi soldiers, killing and injuring almost fifty of them. This caused the Iraqi attack to stall and bought them a little more time until the helicopter arrived. In between the attacks from the F-16, the Iraqis continued to attack the SF team, and on occasions they almost encircled them.

As the battle raged on, they suddenly heard the welcome sound of an American MH-60 Black Hawk helicopter as it approached their position. At last they had arrived. The SF team were expecting a couple of helicopters and where somewhat surprised to see only one. The Black Hawk, flying towards the American position was from the 160th Special Operations Aviation Regiment (SOAR) and was being flown by Chief Warrant Officer James (Monk) Chrisatulli, and his co-pilot, Chief Warrant Officer Randy Stephens. The Black Hawk was rushing down the MSR, at around 140 knots, barely six feet above it. The helicopter was flying parallel to a 20-foot high power line, which if hit, would bring the Black Hawk down. The crew of the helicopter looked around for the SF team, and asked them to fire a flare to mark their position.

The SF team popped a flare and upon seeing it, the Black Hawk crew jumped the power line and flew straight towards their position. The crew then pulled the helicopter's nose into the air, causing it to flare in front of the SF teams position. They then slammed the Black Hawk onto the ground and as they did so the door gunners opened fire on the Iraqis with their miniguns, causing the enemy soldiers to take cover. The SF team rapidly boarded the Black Hawk and under cover of the dust cloud that had been kicked up by the helicopter's rotor-blades, they made good their escape. As they flew down the road, the Iraqis opened fire on the Black Hawk with every weapon available. Although the helicopter was hit in numerous places, it continued to fly and the crew were able to reach friendly lines without any further drama. The Black Hawk helicopter that had performed the dramatic rescue was so badly damaged that it never flew again during the Gulf War. The pilot and co-pilot were both awarded the Distinguished Flying Cross. The leader of the Special Forces team was awarded the Silver Star for Gallantry and the other soldiers involved in this action were awarded the Bronze Star for Valour. This rescue again demonstrated the skill and bravery of the pilots and aircrew of the 160th and greatly enhanced their image within the American Armed Forces, during Operation "Desert Storm".

CHAPTER 5
THE MOTHER OF ALL RAIDS
Mike McKinney

The most memorable events in military history are those which involve bold strokes of genius. Pearl Harbor, Inchon, and Entebbe provide just a few examples of risky, yet highly rewarding attacks that paralyzed the enemy and gave momentum to the attacker. In the opening moments of "Desert Storm" helicopter crews of the 20th Special Operations Squadron and 101st Airborne Division mounted such an attack. The Green Hornets of the 20th SOS were one of the first US units to arrive in Saudi Arabia after the Iraqi invasion of Kuwait. The invasion sent shock waves throughout the world, as the obvious next move for the Iraqis was to continue south into Saudi Arabia. Less than two weeks after the August 2nd 1990 invasion, the first C-5 Galaxy carrying two MH-53J Pave Lows touched down in Dhahran. Just like everyone else in the theatre, the initial 20th crews were unsure as to what to expect and they had to be prepared for anything. The first task was to rebuild the helicopters – a process that takes about a day. Next, living quarters and a planning area needed to be established to prepare for possible missions. Almost immediately, the Green Hornets were tasked to provide alert coverage for SEAL reconnaissance teams near the border and combat search and rescue (CSAR) for air operations. As the weeks went by and the immediate threat from the Iraqi forces waned, a cell of officers was assembled to plan the air campaign that became known as 'Instant Thunder'. Out of this planning cell came an audacious plan to punch a hole in the Iraqi radar network, thereby providing Allied aircraft a pathway into deeper regions of the country. This plan was known as Operation 'Eager Anvil.'

To understand the importance of 'Eager Anvil' it is necessary to study the workings of an integrated air defence system (IADS). The Iraqis built a fairly dense and sophisticated IADS comprised of mostly Soviet and French equipment. The most obvious parts of an IADS are the various SAM and AAA systems. The Iraqi system consisted of medium-range SAMs, like the SA-6 Gainful; long-range SAMs, like the SA-2 Guideline; and numerous AAA pieces of varying sizes. These threat systems provided overlapping coverage against high and low altitude aircraft, making life very difficult for Allied aircrews. The next essential elements of an IADS are the early warning (EW) radars. These high-powered radar systems have the ability to identify and track aircraft hundreds of miles away. Although SAM systems have integral radars, they normally have much smaller ranges, and are used primarily for target intercept and missile guidance. Information gathered by the EW radars provides the 'big picture' – the size and axis of attacking force. This information is then passed down to the SAM operators either by radio or telephone. Organizing this information and controlling which targets will be engaged by which SAMs is the job of the Sector Operations Control (SOC). The SOC is the vital node in an IADS, where the critical decisions are made to maximize the SAM and EW assets available. Even the greenest air tactician can see that knocking out a SOC can cripple the effectiveness of an IADS. On the surface this strategy may seem simple however, SOCs are normally located many miles from the forward edge of the battle area (FEBA). This means that the attackers must first penetrate the SAM and EW coverage before even having a chance at the SOC. To make matters worse, most SOCs are themselves protected by SAMs or AAA and many times covered with tons of steel and concrete, making for difficult targets.

Allied planners knew that in order to maximize the effectiveness of the first wave of attacks, something had to be done to the Iraqi IADS. The targets for this first wave consisted of airfields, communication sites, and Scud missile launch sites all located deep inside Iraq. Fighting through the gauntlet of Iraqi SAMs and AAA was not expected to be a pleasant experience. The first course of action in the plan called for a little tactical deception. Attack routing for the first wave was purposely located in the western portion of the country. Most of the Iraqi defences were centred to the east, near the Iraq, Saudi, and Kuwait border. By attacking to the west the planners hoped they could catch the Iraqi air defences off guard. While this would help out, Iraqi air defences were certain to take their toll on the first wave as they crossed the border. Two EW radar sites were identified just north of the Saudi town of Ar Ar, right in the path of the attack aircraft. Knocking out these radars was the key to protecting the force and became an immediate concern to the planners. One of the planners was Capt Randy O'Boyle, a Pave Low pilot sent to act on behalf of SOF air forces in the theatre. He realized that SOF forces could be used to knock out the EW radars with a high degree of success. Destruction of the radars had to be confirmed prior to the attack aircraft crossing the border. The only way this was possible would be to place someone close enough to confirm their destruction without a shadow of doubt. Capt O'Boyle knew that SOF forces provided this capability. Placing SOF ground troops inside Iraq was a very risky proposition and would certainly not be approved by the overall commander,

General Norman Schwarzkopf. The other option was to attack the sites using helicopters. This presented the best option since the Iraqis would hopefully not be prepared for helicopters to approach at low altitude; instead they would be looking high in the sky for fighters. Due to the remoteness of the desert terrain, the helicopters had to be equipped with Global Positioning System (GPS) equipment to ensure precise navigation. The system determines aircraft position by sensing a time signal from orbiting satellites. By comparing the signals from several different satellites, the system derives a position, accurate to within 50 feet. GPS is easily one of the greatest advances in history and has revolutionized the aviation industry. At the time, GPS was relatively new and a very rare piece of avionics in the military inventory. Only a few aircraft had the system installed with Pave Lows being one of those aircraft. By default, the second plan became reality when the Iraqis moved the radar sites back about 20 miles from the border, making the ground force option unacceptable.

The initial plan called for the Pave Lows to attack the radar sites with their own .50 calibre machine guns. Although the .50 cals used armoured piercing incendiary (API) ammunition, capable of easily penetrating the radar dishes and buildings, this could still not ensure the complete destruction of the sites. The planners went looking for more firepower and found it in the AH-64 Apache. Designed to kill hordes of Soviet tanks in central Europe, the Apache is armed to the teeth with plenty of firepower for the job. At the heart of their system is the AGM-114 Hellfire laser-guided missile, capable of reaching out several miles, therefore allowing the Apaches to stand back and attack 'silently'. There were only two limitations to the Apache. First and foremost, the Apache's navigation system wasn't up to the task of the 'gnat's ass' navigation so critical to Eager Anvil. Since the Apache was designed for a short-range war in Europe, the aircraft and crews did not require such a precise navigation system. Apache crews flew 'nap-of-the-earth' and navigated using maps instead of electronics. This type of navigation is nearly impossible in the desert where the terrain can literally change overnight. Unlike today, portable GPS systems that could have easily solved the problem weren't readily available to strap on to the Apaches. The Doppler navigation system that the Apache did have relied on small radar beams pointed at the ground. These beams measure the speed and direction of movement, and then a computer calculates a position based upon the rate and direction of movement from pre-entered coordinates. Although Doppler systems can be very accurate, they are notorious for 'running off' and inducing huge navigational errors unless they are updated over known positions. Also, the fire control system for the Hellfire missiles required an accurate position prior to calculating a firing solution. Without a prominent known position, the Apaches could not ensure complete success. Once again, in the desert, the only way to determine a position with such a high degree of accuracy is with GPS. This meant that the Pave Lows, using GPS, would lead the Apaches to a point where they could then update their Doppler systems, and consequently update their fire control computers. The second problem with the Apache was its range. Loaded up with a full combat weapons load, the Apache has just over two hours of fuel onboard. The Apaches could fly the mission on internal fuel alone, but it left very little room for error or contingencies. Should the helicopters have to circumnavigate threats or weather, the Apaches would not be able to complete the mission. The first idea was to establish a forward area rearming and refuelling point (FARRP) inside Iraq, where the Apaches could stop and refuel. This was a very risky option and increased the complexity of the entire mission. One of the Apache pilots, Lt Tim DeVito solved the problem by proposing that the helicopters replace one of their 2.75-inch rocket pods with a 230 gallon external fuel tank. These tanks were intended for use only on ferry flights and the thought of losing firepower was not appealing to all. Common sense prevailed in the end and the external tanks were placed on the left inboard weapons pylon. If went as planned, the rockets would not be needed anyway. Just to be sure, the Pave Low crews devised an emergency plan to refuel the Apaches by attaching a length of fire hose to the fuel dump tubes of the Pave Lows. The Paves could activate their dump pumps and refuel the Apaches in this very unorthodox way. This would be very risky if utilized and everyone involved hoped this emergency plan would never come to fruition.

Even as the plan was being finalized, the crews selected for the mission were brought together to start rehearsing. Four Pave Low crews and eight Apache crews began training in early October as Task Force Normandy. Because it was still unknown when the air war would begin, it was imperative that the crews quickly worked out the details. Leading the Pave Lows was Lt Col Richard Comer, the squadron commander. Comer was a member of a combat rescue squadron during Vietnam, and participated in the *Mayaguez* rescue mission. As the 20th squadron commander, he not only chose the crews to fly the mission but also would fly himself as the mission commander. The Apaches were also lead by another warrior, Lt Col Dick Cody, 1st Battalion commander. Like Comer, Cody would also lead by example and fly on the mission. To preserve the secrecy of the mission, the crews were not told the actual targets, or the timing of the raid. Comer and Cody knew the secret to success was in making the different crews work together as one.

A building block approach was taken to the training flights. The crews first practised basic formation skills, learning each other's capabilities and limitations. Night no-communications procedures were practised over and over until the crews could predict the moves of the other helicopters. Live-fire missions were flown on gunnery ranges so the Apaches could refine their attack runs and decide which weapons to use. Each step in the training was undertaken in a very careful and detailed manner. By December, the crews were divided into two teams, *Red* and *White*; each tasked with attacking a different radar site. As Christmas approached, the situation remained unchanged, and the threat of war grew ever greater. Task Force Normandy had sharpened their skills to a fine edge. The deadline set by President Bush for Iraqi troops to leave Kuwait was now only a couple of weeks away. By now the crews knew what the targets were but still had no idea that they would strike the first blow of the war.

In the early weeks of January the crews were finally told the details of the mission. Gen. Schwarzkopf approved the mission only on the assurance of 100 percent success, now it was up to the men of Task Force Normandy to make it happen. The final training flight was flown on 10 January. Actual timing and flight distances were flown during this flight providing one last chance to identify any problems and fix them. On 14 January, the crews deployed to Al Jouf, Saudi Arabia, a barren forward operating location located about 130 miles south of the Iraqi border. During the afternoon of the 16 January, the final decision was made on the timing of the raid; the war would start that night. The crews were told to get some rest and write a letter home, just in case things turned bad. Everyone wrote letters and few got any sleep. At 2100 hours a final briefing was held to pass last minute details to the crews. The tension and seriousness of the mission was evident on the faces of everyone in the room.

On 16 January, at 2330 hours, the crews arrived at the helicopters and began the pre-flight checklists. Engines were started one hour later and all the systems checked and rechecked to ensure everything was working properly. A perfectly working helicopter is absolutely essential when going into combat. White team would take off first – their target was the eastern-most radar site and required them to fly farther. Capt Mike Kingsley, *White* team flight lead, lifted his Pave Low off the ground at 0113 hours, on his wing was Maj Bob Leonik and Lt Col Comer in the second MH-53J. Capt Corby Martin, *Red* team flight lead, departed seven minutes later enroute to the western target. The second Pave Low in *Red* team was lead by Maj Ben Pulsifer. The two flights weaved around any ground lighting they saw to remain as covert as possible. The crews noticed how different the terrain was in the western region of the country. All of the training flights took place in the east where the terrain resembles a sandy, flat beach. In the west however, the terrain becomes quite hilly with numerous wadis, or dry riverbeds. This played perfectly into their plans since the helicopters could get down low in the wadis and terrain mask. At 0212, the first Pave Low crossed the Iraqi border right on time – there was no turning back now.

The flight to the initial point was much shorter than the flight to the border. About 20 miles inside Iraq, the Pave Lows had reached the initial point. Using a predetermined signal, dropping a bundle of green chemical lights taped together, Capt Kingsley's helicopter marked the point for the following Apaches. The Paves made a sharp 180-degree turn and proceeded to the holding point to watch the show. All four Apaches pulled up on the chem lights and updated their coordinates. In their forward looking infrared (FLIR) video screens the radar sites could clearly be seen in the distance. The Apaches continued forward toward their targets. About two miles away and precisely at 0238 hours, the Apaches opened fire with their Hellfire missiles. In the FLIR videotapes, an Iraqi soldier standing guard outside can be seen running toward the site, and just as he opens the door a Hellfire impacts the building. Within seconds, the Apaches continue the attack with 2.75in rockets and 30mm rounds from their guns. The radar site explodes into a huge fireball, lighting up the desert for miles around. Simultaneously, *Red* team attacks the farthest site in similar fashion. Intelligence assets immediately notice the disappearance of radar signals from the sites. The men in the helicopters didn't need any reassurance that the sites were destroyed, they could see it with their own eyes. The war had started and Task Force Normandy had struck the first blow.

Although the mission was complete, the war was just beginning and the Pave Lows had to prepare for their next mission. Planners predicted that a large number of aircraft would be shot down during the first night. The use of four Paves on Eager Anvil put a huge dent in the ability to conduct CSAR missions. As a result, Task Force Normandy's primary mission became CSAR coverage after the attacks. The crews could see numerous fighters south of the border streaming northward. As they neared the border, the fighters extinguished their position lights and streaked toward their targets through the hole Normandy had just produced. Small arms fire came up from the desert at the Pave Lows and Apaches as they made their way to the border. Suddenly, an SA-7 infrared missile flashed toward Martin's helicopter. Martin turned hard and dove toward the desert. The missile streaked by the Pave Low, decoyed by the infrared countermeasures system located on top of the external fuel tanks. Without this system the missile would probably have found its mark. From that distance, the reaction time to evade a missile is measured in milliseconds. All of the helicopters of Task Force Normandy made it safely across the border and awaited the next mission. For the Apaches that meant a month and a half wait for the ground war to begin. The Pave Lows air-refuelled from waiting HC-130P tankers in order to have plenty of loiter time available for CSAR taskings. Luckily none came, and the crews recovered back to Al Jouf around 0500 hours, tired but still anxious from what they had just accomplished.

Operation 'Eager Anvil' was just a small part of a much larger air war yet the impact of the mission had far reaching implications. It is impossible to predict how many aircrafts were saved because of the destruction of the radar sites. 'Eager Anvil' was an overwhelming success and exhibited many of the same tenets of special operations missions. Completely different crews were brought together for the mission, a common thread with other historic missions. These crews trained for several months, preparing and honing their skills to a fine edge. The importance of this training cannot be overemphasized as it builds the basis for success. During this time the planners and crews critiqued and modified the plan leaving no stone unturned. The mission has also shown that a unit does not have to be a full-time SOF unit to participate in a special operations mission. The skills needed are inherent to nearly every helicopter unit in the military and can easily be developed should the need arise. Details of the mission remained close-hold for several years later even to members of the units involved. In another ironic twist, in the

October 1991 issue of Air Force Magazine, an article about the mission detailed the Apaches involvement, but only briefly mentioned the Pave Lows contribution. Because of the uniqueness of the mission and the ingenuity of the participants, 'Eager Anvil' has gone down in military history as a striking example of the unique capabilities SOF provides to the overall campaign.

CHAPTER 6
SLATE 46 IS DOWN
Mike McKinney

For Navy Lieutenants Devon Jones and Larry Slade, 21 January 1991 was not a good day. They were flying their first combat mission over the skies of Iraq; unaware that it would also be their last. The mission for *Slate 46* was to escort an EA-6B Prowler electronic warfare aircraft in the vicinity of Al Asad airfield. A strike package was attacking the airfield just before daylight and the EA-6B was there to attack any air defence batteries. Lt Jones and Lt Slade were flying an F-14A Tomcat from the carrier *USS Saratoga*. Everything seemed to be working according to plan until an SA-2 Guideline SAM streaked toward the F-14. Jones immediately tried to counter the missile but to no avail. The SA-2 detonated behind the F-14, sending it spiralling out of control. At about 14,000 feet, Jones and Slade ejected and became the eleventh combat loss of the war.

The job of Combat Search and Rescue (CSAR) for "Desert Storm" fell on the shoulders of the US Air Force Special Operations Command (AFSOC). Air Rescue Service (ARS), the Air Force agency normally dedicated to CSAR, was caught in a delicate situation as it transitioned to new helicopters. ARS was not in a position to deploy for combat operations, which dropped the CSAR ball in AFSOC's lap. The units organized under AFSOC were heavily tasked right from the beginning of the air campaign planning. Due to the lack of available heli-copters, the Army's 160th Special Operations Aviation Regiment

(SOAR) was also tasked to provide CSAR coverage. The basic CSAR plan was developed in August, immediately after the first AFSOC forces arrived in theatre. By October, the plan was finalized by Capt Randy O'Boyle and Capt Tim Minish. They developed an intricate network of 'spider routes'; predetermined points laid out on a map of Iraq to use as quick reference points. Probably the most difficult part of the plan was the coordination required among all the players in a CSAR mission. AFSOC helicopters rarely trained with conventional USAF aircraft and both sides were unfamiliar with the capabilities and limitations of each other. Conducting CSAR exercises (CSAREX) ironed out these details. Each CSAREX varied in scope and complexity, allowing for creative thought and critique of the overall plan. The 20th SOS would provide coverage for the southern region of the country while the 21st SOS would cover the north, both flying the MH-53J Pave Low IIIE. Augmenting these squadrons were MH-60Gs of the 55th SOS, MH-3s of the 71st SOS, MH-60Ls of the 160th SOAR and Navy HH-60Hs of HCS-4 and HCS-5. By December, the CSAR forces were trained and prepared for the air war to commence. The remaining question was whether they would be task-saturated on the first day. Many pessimistic estimates claimed that the Iraqi IADS would take a heavy toll on Allied aircraft. There was some worry that there would not be enough CSAR helicopters to conduct the missions. Luckily this never came to be a reality.

The first chance for CSAR came on 19 January, as an F-16 was shot down near Talil Airfield in southern Iraq. Two MH-53Js launched and searched the area for several minutes. Poor weather forced the Pave Lows to penetrate the Iraqi IADS using their terrain following/terrain avoidance (TF/TA) radar system. Unfortunately, they never made contact with any survivors and were forced to head back to Saudi Arabia without success. Another mission was flown the very next day but was again unsuccessful. With little place to hide in the desert, downed aviators were easy prey for Iraqi captors. The other early lesson of the war was that it was much more difficult to locate survivors than previously imagined. On 21 January, these same problems surfaced again, but the results would be different.

Sitting alert for CSAR coverage that day were Capt Tom Trask and Maj Mike Homan. When the word came that *Slate 46* was down in Iraq, both men were trying to get some much-needed rest. *Slate 46's* position was plotted to be about 60 miles north-west of Baghdad, nearly 130 miles inside Iraq. After some initial planning and coordinating, *Moccasin 05* departed Ar' Ar airfield at 0805 hours. The weather was less than optimal, thick fog hugged the terrain. This would be an advantage for Trask and Homan. The fog would make it difficult for Iraqi gunners to see the Pave Low. *Moccasin 05* pressed for the border, and almost on cue the fog lifted as they crossed into enemy territory. Now they would have to fly the Pave Low as low as possible to mask from the air defence batteries. A large Pave Low, flying around in a daylight desert environment, is just about in the worst situation possible. About 50 miles into Iraq, an orbiting E-3 Airborne Warning and Control (AWACS) aircraft sent out an alert to *Moccasin 05* that an Iraqi MiG-23 fighter was flying in their direction. Unable to outrun the fighter, the crew continued on towards the coordinates. The Pave Low arrived in the area at 0815 and started searching for Jones and Slade. After about 25 minutes the determination was made that either the crew had been captured or the coordinates were wrong. As fuel became a factor, Trask and Homan headed back to the south to refuel.

At about 1200 hours *Sandy 57*, one of the A-10 RESCORT fighters, finally made contact with Jones. He was uninjured and had buried himself in a makeshift foxhole. At the same time, *Moccasin 05* was being refuelled back at Ar' Ar. Trask and Homan got the word that at least one of the crew had been located. This marked the first time since the start of the war that a downed aviator had actually been located. The crew of *Moccasin 05* knew that if they could get to the area quickly, the chance for success was great. As soon as the refuelling was complete, the Pave Lows departed and once again 'crossed the fence' signalling entry into enemy territory. It was evident that the Iraqis were aware of the CSAR mission and they were desperately trying to locate Jones by 'Dfing' his position. This meant that the Iraqis were monitoring his survival radio transmissions and using equipment to determine the location of the source. Now it was simply a race to determine whether *Moccasin 05* or the Iraqis would get to Jones first. Overhead were several A-10s and other fighters determined to ensure that no Iraqis would even get close to the downed aviator. As the Pave Low approached, the A-10s asked for Jones to confirm his exact location. He stated that he was about 1000 yards due east of a large blue water tank. More proof of the Iraqis monitoring occurred as almost immediately a military truck was spotted heading straight for Jones. Obviously, they were listening to everything and knew about the water tank. Everyone involved in the mission spotted the truck, Jones, the A-10s and the crew of *Moccasin 05*. In seconds one of the A-10 pilots rolled in and let loose with his 30mm cannon. The truck was shot down less than 150 yards away from Jones. *Moccasin 05* landed right next to Jones. He uncovered himself from his desert hide and raced to the helicopter. Fortunately the egress out of Iraq was uneventful and *Moccasin 05* recovered back to Al Jouf Airbase. The crew of *Moccasin 05* had just logged the first combat rescue mission since Vietnam.

The remainder of the short war saw two more successful CSAR missions, one flown by the 160th SOAR and one by a Navy destroyer-based SH-60. In total, 43 US and Allied aircraft were lost during 'Desert Storm' with only three successful CSAR missions. On the surface this looks like a pitiful record but the circumstances surrounding the shoot-downs has to be considered. Many of the aircraft were downed in the daylight and close to Iraqi troops. The desert environment leaves little chance for concealment. As a pilot floats down in his parachute he makes for an easy target. All the Iraqi troops had to do was wait for the pilot to land. Early in the war another CSAR attempt was made by MH-53J Pave Lows from the 21st SOS flying out of Batman, Turkey. *Corvette 03* was an F-15E Strike Eagle shot down near Baghdad. The crew evaded for over a day but political problems prevented their successful recovery. Because of their location, the Pave Lows would have to transit Syrian airspace to conduct the mission. Initially the Syrians denied the request and it took several days to gain permission. By the time the Pave Lows finally launched and conducted the search, the crew of *Corvette 03* had already been captured.

The role of SOF helicopters in 'Desert Storm' was crucial to the overall campaign. From the first strike on opening night, to hunting SCUD missiles, to CSAR, SOF helicopters proved that a small force can cause devastating effects on the battlefield. This in essence is the major benefit to using SOF. The missions that SOF are tasked to perform are usually high-risk and high-reward. Failure can have disastrous consequences yet success can turn the tide of a war. 'Desert Storm' further cemented the role of SOF helicopters in overall campaign planning. Since the end of the war, SOF helicopters and ground forces have been the 'go to' units within the military.

CHAPTER 7
HAWKS DOWN
Mike Ryan

America's Armed Forces were left with a feeling of euphoria at the end of the Gulf War. At long last they had laid the ghosts of Vietnam to rest and they could once again walk tall in the eyes of the American Public. America now saw itself as a Global Policeman, ready to take on the role of peacemaker and peacekeeper. Its Armed Forces were the best equipped in the World, and its success during the Gulf War gave the impression that nothing could again upset the American military status quo.

However after "Desert Storm", nobody would ever have believed that a small third world country in Eastern Africa would have the ability to inflict a serious military crisis on America's armed forces. Especially as their main weapons only consisted of AK-47 Rifles, 12.7mm machine guns and Rocket Propelled Grenades (RPG). The country in question was Somalia – a poverty stricken land that had been at war with itself for decades. If asked, most Americans would not have been able to locate it on a map. That was until 1991, when the American Embassy in Mogadishu, Somalia, was threatened by groups of ill-disciplined, highly dangerous armed bandits. In response America sent a small task force of SEALs, and US Marines, by CH-53 helicopters, to secure the Embassy compound. This Force was sent in advance of a larger Task Force that was on its way to evacuate the Embassy staff. Eventually the American ships arrived off the coast of Somalia, and began the evacuation. As the USMC CH-53s shuttled back and forth, from the ships to the Embassy compound, they started to come under enemy sniper fire. Fortunately it was ineffective and no American casualties were taken, although America had just experienced its first taste of Somalia.

On 9 December 1992, American Forces again returned to Somalia, this time for humanitarian operations. Somalia was in the grip of a major famine that threatened the lives of thousands of innocent people. The crisis in Somalia, had been caused by years of political chaos and non-stop warring by the armed Somali war lords, who terrorized the country. World leaders decided to take action before a major humanitarian disaster occurred. As a result, a major operation was mounted to secure major air and sea-ports, key installations and food distribution points in order to facilitate the free passage of relief supplies threatened by armed warlords. This operation was named 'Restore Hope', and involved forces from over 23 different countries.

America had already experienced Somalia in 1990, during Operation 'Eastern Exit'; when under enemy gunfire, they evacuated 281 citizens from over thirty nations. This time they arrived in Somalia prepared for trouble. The Marines stormed ashore, in strength, on the beaches of Mogadishu. They wanted to make sure that the warlords saw them arriving; the strategy being that the might of the American armed forces on show in front of them might make them think twice about confrontation. That was the theory, however America had underestimated the Somalis and their appetite for war. This was a country that knew little else but war, so for them death held no fear. America and its allies in Somalia totalled 38,000 troops including 12,000 Marines. Air assets comprised of Marine Cobra gunships and

USAF AC-130 Spectre gunships, supported by Marine CH-53s
and MH-60 Black Hawks from the US Army 160th SOAR.

The initial stages of 'Restore Hope', involved stabilizing the
country's infrastructure. In addition to weapon sweeps, and
convoy escorts, UNITAF (United Task Forces) pursued extensive
civic action programmes including repairing more than 1200
miles of roads, drilling wells, and rebuilding hospitals and
schools. UNITAF personnel also treated Somalis for diseases,
such as Typhoid and Malaria, though their main work was the
treatment of gunshot wounds. America realized that if there
were to be a lasting peace in Somalia, the warlords would have
to be removed.

In June 1993, America turned over its peacekeeping responsibilities in Somalia to the UN. Around the same time, a local
warlord named Mohammed Aideed decided to launch a major
campaign to strengthen his political and military position in
Mogadishu, Somalia's capital. Frustrating Aideed's campaign of
terror and intimidation, was a detachment of Pakistani United
Nations soldiers, who had been patrolling the streets of
Mogadishu around Aideed's neighbourhood, in an attempt to
restore public confidence. Aideed, did not take kindly to the UN
actions, and ordered his armed thugs to attack the Pakistani
troops. On 12 June 1993, Aideed's Forces attacked the UN
soldiers as they patrolled the streets. During the fighting, twenty-
four soldiers were killed and many more wounded. This attack
shocked both America and the UN, and revenge quickly followed. America responded with attacks on Aideed's residence
and his nearby military compound, using AC-130 Spectre gunships. For over eighteen hours, US helicopters and aircraft
methodically took apart Aideed's military empire, forcing him
into hiding. American Forces launched a ground operation in an

attempt to find Aideed, however his Somali supporters had hidden him well and all that was found were the bodies of four Somalis killed the night before.

It had become clear that ordinary soldiers were not enough to deter the warlords from attacking the UN. The only thing that the warlords understood was force, so as a result the US deployed Ranger soldiers to stabilize Mogadishu. During the summer of 1993, over 400 Rangers were deployed to Somalia, along with elements of the 160th SOAR, as part of Task Force Ranger. The Operation was part of Operation UNOSOM 2 in support of the United Nations in Somalia. Upon their arrival in Mogadishu, Somalia, the Rangers and the 160th lost no time in putting their mark on the city. Throughout the hot African Summer, the Black Hawk helicopters of the 160th orbited the Somali capital like Eagles soaring above a Canyon. Flying above Mogadishu, or 'Mog', as it was nicknamed by American forces. The Rangers and their Black Hawk helicopters seemed almost detached from the chaos that was going on below them.

They were however, unknowingly, creating a time-bomb that was going to explode on them in the near future. As the Rangers flew above the Somali people, many of them had taken to sitting in the door entrance of their Black Hawk helicopters, in an attempt to try and keep cool by using the down draft from the helicopters rotor-blades. In itself, this was an innocent enough act, however, as they sat in the doorways, they dangled their feet outside of the helicopters, showing the soles of their boots to the Somalis below. They didn't know it, but this was the ultimate insult that you could give a Somali. As a result, every time the Rangers' Black Hawks passed over the crowds in the markets and streets below, they were insulting the ordinary people of

Mogadishu. This was to have a disastrous effect on American and UN operations, because the very people that they had come to assist, were now turning against them and siding with the warlords instead.

On 3 October 1993, an incident occurred in Mogadishu that was to leave America's military and political leaders traumatised. Before this fateful date, American intelligence sources had located Aideed and three of his Lieutenants, hiding in a house on Hawlwadig road. America had a number of Somali spies on its payroll. Their role was to report on the movements of known warlords, and their Lieutenants. They were however, notoriously unreliable, and many of their alleged sightings were later proven to be false. As a result of these unreliable intelligence reports, many planned attacks involving both the Rangers and the 160th SOAR were cancelled just before mission execution. So when the order came to mount up for another operation to arrest Aideed and his Lieutenants, the Rangers were a little dubious of its authenticity.

The afternoon of Sunday 3 October 1993 was different. This time the Rangers and Delta Force were going downtown. They were going to launch a combined operation against the target house in Hawlwadig road and although Aideed's presence couldn't be guaranteed, they new that many of his Lieutenants used it as a regular meeting point, so they were assured of capturing some of Mogadishu's more active warlords. The mission had been deemed a snatch and grab operation and would involve nineteen aircraft, twelve vehicles and some 160 Ranger and Delta Force personnel. The mission planners were well aware of the fact that the target house was located in a very pro-Aideed area, so some resistance was possible. The task force that was being sent in was the best in the business, and they were not frightened or intimidated by the Somalis in any way. These were men that lived for danger. Danger came with the territory, and today was going to be 'Judgement Day'.

The plan was that four Ranger chalks would be inserted in and around the target house area. Once deployed, each chalk would take up a position on the comer of the block that contained the target house. As the target area was being sealed, Delta Force would storm the house and capture everyone inside. On completion of the operation, the Ranger Force and Delta, along with its prisoners, would be taken back to base via ground vehicles that would rendezvous (RV) at the target house at the same time as the helicopter's arrival. Estimated time for execution of Operation 'Irene' – one hour.

Waiting to go on the tarmac were four AH-6 Little Birds. These were small, highly agile two-seater helicopters that packed a large punch with their armament of rockets and mini-guns. The operation called for two Little Birds to make an initial sweep over the target house, with the other two providing defence at the rear of the Air Assault group. There were four MH-6 Little Birds, fitted with benches mounted on both sides of the helicopter for inserting the spearhead of the assault force, Delta Force's C Squadron. In addition to the small helicopters, there were eight Black Hawks. These belonged to the 160th SOAR and were tasked with bringing in the bulk of the assault force. Two were assigned to the Delta Force assault team and their ground command unit. Four were assigned to Ranger Company B, 3rd Battalion of the Army's 75th Infantry Division. One carried a CSAR (Combat Search and Rescue) team. While the other one carried two mission commanders: Lt Col Tom Matthews, the coordinating officer for the 160th, and Delta Force commander Lt Col Gary Harrell, who was responsible for all of the men on the ground (including the ground convoy) that would RV at the target house.

At the front of the base, the ground convoy was formed up awaiting the order to move out. The convoy consisted of nine wide-body Humvees and three five-ton trucks, for transporting the prisoners and Assault force team back to base upon completion of the mission. Above the ground convoy and Air Assault group, were three additional OH-58 observation helicopters that were equipped with video cameras and radio relay equipment, that could relay the mission as it happened back to the Joint Operations Centre (JOC). Taking overall command of the mission was an Navy Orion surveillance plane. This aircraft had been flying high above the streets of Mogadishu for weeks, gathering information and data that could be used by both America and the UN. Its exact capabilities were highly classified, however it was known to carry sophisticated surveillance equipment that could relay mission performances back to the Pentagon as they happened.

As the air armada sat on the airbase tarmac with their engines running, a signal reached all of the helicopters, "IRENE". This was their cue to begin. The helicopters climbed into the sky and headed towards the target area in Mogadishu. They flew parallel to the Indian Ocean, until they reached the outskirts of the capital, then they banked hard to port in a Westerly direction towards the target house. The armada flew in a rough crescent formation, very low and very fast. As they swept in towards the target house in Hawlwadig road, the Somalis on the ground began to scatter in all directions. They knew that a helicopter force of this size meant only one thing: trouble.

As the Little Bird and Black Hawk helicopters took up their insertion positions, they started to come under enemy fire. At this stage it was mostly ineffective and it was a situation that everyone was prepared for. As the helicopters flared for their approach to the target house, huge clouds of dust were being kicked up, which made judging position difficult. On one occasion an MH-6 almost landed on top of another helicopter that had landed in the wrong place due to the dust whirling around beneath him. So far the mission was proceeding according to plan – the Delta team had stormed the house without any problems and were in the process of rounding up the prisoners. Outside the house, medics were treating one of the soldiers who had been critically injured during the insertion. He had dropped more than seventy feet from a hovering helicopter after missing the insertion rope, and desperately needed to be evacuated back to base for surgery.

The mission around the house was virtually complete. All that was needed now was the arrival of the transport convoy. Outside the house, the intensity of the shooting was increasing dramatically, word having got out around Mogadishu about the American assault and just about every Somali in the area had turned up to fight with them. In most countries, once the shooting starts, the innocent disappear, leaving the combatants to fight it out. However in Somalia the sounds of gunfire attracted everyone. This made the situation for the American soldiers even harder then expected, as they were taking heavy fire and were finding it difficult to return fire without hitting young children and elderly folk who were amongst the gunmen.

The 160th had originally wanted to perform this mission at night, as their night time flying skills were well developed, hence their nickname – Night Stalkers. There was also another good reason for night time operations, a drug called Khat was popular with some of the Somalis, which usually knocked them out in the evening, making them very vulnerable to attack. There seems to have been many good and viable reasons for a night assault and both the 160th SOAR and their Ranger passengers would have preferred this to an attack in broad daylight. It would seem that the decision to go with a daylight assault had more to do with publicity and the fact that the JOC could watch it on their television screens in colour, as it happened. The fact that three camera-equipped helicopters took part in this operation seems to back up this theory.

The 160th SOAR, along with the Ranger and Delta teams, had already performed six snatch-and-grab missions before the one on 3 October. Five had been totally successful, however one had been a PR disaster for the American Forces, due to the fact that UN personnel were snatched instead of Somali warlords. This incident was as much the fault of the UN as it was the United States, however the press didn't see this and chose to remember the one failed mission, rather than those that were successful. This may be the key reason for an assault during the day, rather than at night, because all of the world's media would be watching.

The American Forces had always varied their methods of insertion and extraction, so that the Somalis could not predict the order of the operation. They would sometimes arrive by helicopter, but leave by vehicle, or arrive by helicopter and leave by helicopter. Either way there was no set operational template, for the Somalis to adapt their tactics. This was of the utmost importance, as the Somalis had shown themselves to be aggressive and tenacious opponents in combat. They were also very adept at modifying existing weapons or equipment for other purposes. They had found a way of changing the warheads on their RPGs (Rocket Propelled Grenade) so that they could be used against low flying helicopters. They also operated a unique type of vehicle, known locally as a 'Technical'. These were basic pick-up trucks, normally Toyotas, which had 12.7mm machine guns mounted on the flat deck, behind the vehicle's cab. Although very crude, they were remarkably effective, and were seen by the Somali warlords as a status symbol.

Because of the recent American successes against the warlords, there was a ruthless determination by the Somalis to inflict a significant military set-back upon them – just as they had done against the Pakistani UN soldiers. The Somalis knew that the Americans were very cautious about casualties. By killing just a few of them, it would be enough to cause severe political problems for the Clinton administration back in Washington, and without American support for the UN mission in Somalia, Operation 'Restore Hope' would collapse.

By now the convoy carrying the assault force and Somali prisoners was making its way slowly across Mogadishu. They were taking fire from just about every direction, and it was only a matter of time before the Somalis forced them to a halt. Realizing what the Somalis were trying to do, helicopters of the 160th started to orbit the convoy and lay down suppressive fire on the warlords and their militias. They were however, playing into the Somalis hands, as they had positioned a number of their men around the convoy, who were armed with RPGs. In front of the convoy a Black Hawk helicopter, callsign *Super Six-One*, was flying low over the city in an attempt to draw the Somalis fire. In the back of the helicopter, four Delta snipers were doing their best to take out mob leaders, who were gathering in the streets in an attempt to stop the convoy.

As *Super Six-One* moved towards the eastern part of Mogadishu, an observer in one of the other helicopters spotted a

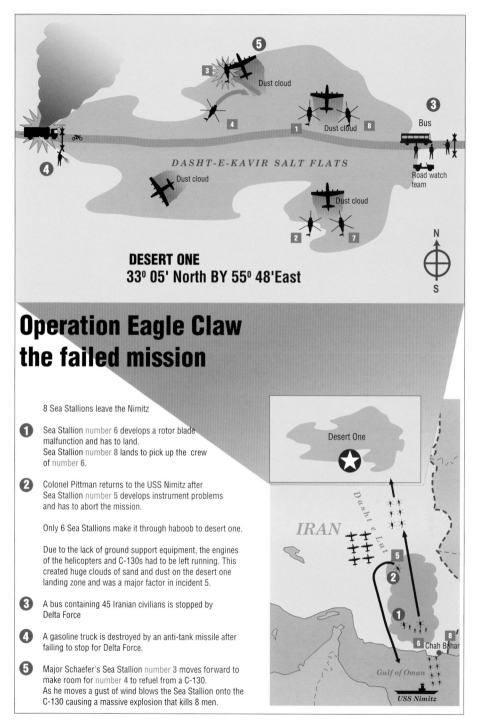

Dust cloud

3

5

Dust cloud

4

1

Dust cloud

8

Bus

3

DASHT-E-KAVIR SALT FLATS

4

Dust cloud

Road watch
team

Dust cloud

2

7

DESERT ONE
33° 05' North BY 55° 48'East

N

S

Operation Eagle Claw
the failed mission

Desert One

IRAN

8 Sea Stallions leave the Nimitz

1 Sea Stallion number 6 develops a rotor blade
malfunction and has to land.
Sea Stallion number 8 lands to pick up the crew
of number 6.

2 Colonel Pittman returns to the USS Nimitz after
Sea Stallion number 5 develops instrument problems
and has to abort the mission.

Only 6 Sea Stallions make it through haboob to desert one.

Due to the lack of ground support equipment, the engines
of the helicopters and C-130s had to be left running. This
created huge clouds of sand and dust on the desert one
landing zone and was a major factor in incident 5.

3 A bus containing 45 Iranian civilians is stopped by
Delta Force

4 A gasoline truck is destroyed by an anti-tank missile after
failing to stop for Delta Force.

5 Major Schaefer's Sea Stallion number 3 moves forward to
make room for number 4 to refuel from a C-130.
As he moves a gust of wind blows the Sea Stallion onto the
C-130 causing a massive explosion that kills 8 men.

Dasht e Lut

5

2

1

6 Chah Bahar

8

Gulf of Oman

USS Nimitz

A diagram detailing the factors which led to the failure of Operation 'Eagle Claw' in
Iran. (AVPRO)

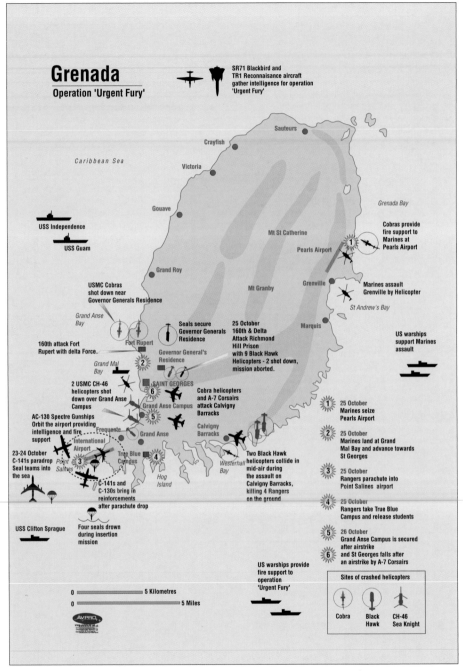

A diagram describing the events of Operation 'Urgent Fury' in Grenada. (AVPRO)

Capt. Jeb Seagle and Capt. Tim Howard pictured here in front of their AH-1T Cobra Gunship, along with other aircrew prior to the Grenada deployment in 1983. (USMC)

US Marines storm the beach at Grand Anse Campus during Operation 'Urgent Fury.' (AVPRO)

A bullet-riddled USMC CH-46 lies on the Grand Anse beach after being hit during the 1983 Grenada operation. (USMC)

Photographed by a tourist, just seconds before crashing into the sea, this USMC Cobra Gunship was shot down off the coast of Grenada during Operation 'Urgent Fury' in 1983. Tragically both crew members were killed. (US DOD)

The Osprey Tilt-Rotor. A cross between an aircraft and a helicopter will give the US Armed Forces a totally new operational capability. (USAF)

The shape of things to come. The AVPRO Titan CRW (Canard Rotor Wing) is one of many concepts that are being offered to the US Armed Forces for future operational requirements. (AVPRO)

USAF MH-53s, equipped with sophisticated navigational aids, lead Army Apache attack helicopters into action on the first night of Operation 'Desert Storm.' Note the lightsticks that have been dropped as a forming-up marker. (R. Wong)

An Exint Pod carried by an Apache attack helicopter at the UK Boscombe Down Defence Facility. The AVPRO EXINT (Extraction/Insertion) Pod is a personnel or equipment carrying capsule, designed for CSAR and Special Operations. It can be carried by any modern attack helicopter and in the case of the Apache, up to four can be mounted on the underwing stores pylons. (DERA)

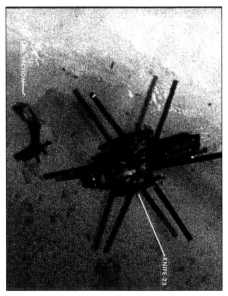 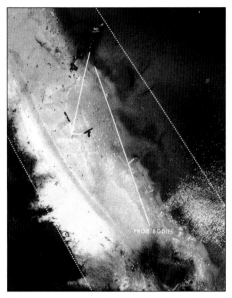

Taken the day after the assault, this photograph shows the wreckage of one of the USAF HH-53s shot down as it deployed US Marines on the island of Koh Tang. (USAF)

A reconnaissance photograph shows the after-math of the Koh Tang island assault, where 15 US Marines were killed, In 1998 the Vietnamese Government granted permission for the remains of the soldiers to be recovered. (USAF)

A dramatic painting by Ronald Wong captures the shooting down of a USAF HH-53 during the assault on Koh Tang. (R. Wong)

USAF aircraft and helicopters form up for the Son Tay raid. (USAF)

US special forces storm the POW camp at Son Tay. (R Wong)

plume of smoke rising from a Cactus garden below. It was an RPG launch, and before he had a chance to shout a warning, *Super Six-One* had been hit. The pilot, Chief Warrant Officer Cliff Wolcott, known as to his colleagues as Elvis, tried in vain to keep the Black Hawk in the air, however it was too late and the helicopter had gone into a spin and was heading for the ground. The helicopter hit the top of a house and flipped over, landing in a small alley on its side. The Somalis were now descending, on all sides of the crashed helicopter.

Above *Super Six-One*, an observation helicopter had filmed the incident, and was relaying the images back to JOC. As the horrified commanders watched the dreadful scene on their TV screens, they spotted some movement in the helicopter wreckage, and realized that at least some of the occupants had survived the crash. They immediately gave the order for the Ranger and Delta convoy to be diverted towards the crash site to rescue the survivors. The convoy was struggling to make any headway, as the Somalis had dug trenches and built barricades across the streets to impede their progress. The Rangers decided to send 75 men on foot towards the crash site, in a bid to secure it, until the arrival of the vehicles.

Near to the crash scene, the crew of Little Bird, *Star Four-One*, piloted by Chief Warrant Officers Keith Jones and Karl Maier, decided that they were going to land near to the crash site and attempt a rescue. This was an incredibly courageous act, as they were surrounded by hundreds of Somalis baying for their blood and to land amongst them was going to take a lot of nerve, as well as excellent flying skills. These Little Bird pilots, were the cream of the 160th. During Operation 'Just Cause' in Panama, they had earned a lot of respect from the Special Forces, due to their excellent flying skills.

As Jones and Maier orbited the crash scene, they spotted a small area in between two buildings that would make a good landing site, as it provided some degree of protection from the Somali gunmen. The other choice was to make a landing on a nearby road intersection, however this was ruled out, because of the fact that they would be exposed to enemy gunfire from four different sides. The landing area that they had picked was very small, and only a highly skilled pilot, such as a Night Stalker, would be able to land there.

With good judgement they skilfully manoeuvred the Little Bird into the gap between the buildings and landed. As they jumped out of their helicopter, a group of Rangers approached from behind them, and proceeded to secure the area. Some of the Rangers looked on in amazement, finding it unbelievable that a helicopter could land in such a small space. The pressure soon began to increase as the Somalis were beginning to regroup for another attack on the crashed helicopter site. Jones and Maier had found two survivors at the crash site, who were in urgent need of medical attention. With the help of the Rangers they put them on board the Little Bird and left the carnage of *Super Six- One* behind.

The American forces were now feeling extremely vulnerable, the loss of *Super Six-One* had really hit them hard and they knew that if they didn't get out of Aideed's neighbourhood fast, there would be many more casualties. The vehicle convoy was being shot to pieces from all sides and they still hadn't reached the site of the crashed Black Hawk. Overhead, confusion reigned, the Orion spy plane was desperately trying to direct the lost convoy – however there was a major communications problem. The Orion was unable to talk to the convoy directly, instead any instructions that they had, needed to be passed through the JOC and this took time. So if they told the convoy to take a left turn at the next intersection, by the time this instruction had been through the chain of command, the convoy would have long passed the turning. As a result the convoy was in danger, due to the appalling indecisiveness of the JOC. The Rangers in the convoy were rapidly losing confidence in their command and control system, and only the fact that they were a highly disciplined unit kept them together.

All around Mogadishu, the Somali gunmen were rallying to the call to kill the Americans. Killing American soldiers on the ground wasn't enough for the Somalis, they knew that the best way to hurt the Americans was to shoot down a helicopter. They had already brought one down today and they were now looking for number two. The Somalis had received guidance in shooting down helicopters from fundamentalists who had fought in Afghanistan. They had discovered that by removing the detonators from the RPG warheads, and replacing them with timing devices, they could make them explode in mid-air. That way they would not need a direct hit to cripple a helicopter. They had also developed very simple, but effective tactics for anti-helicopter operations. They learnt to wait until one passed over and to shoot up at it from behind. The shooter was taught to lie on his back with the RPG firing tube pointing into the ground, he would then cover himself with foliage or a robe, until the helicopter passed overhead. At that moment he would fire the RPG, and then take cover.

The Somalis had become experts with the RPGs and already had victim number two in their sights. Flying in Black Hawk, *Super Six-Four*, was Chief Warrant Officer Mike Durant. He had just joined the action and was in the process of providing fire-support to the Rangers below him, when he suddenly felt a small shudder through the airframe of his helicopter. An RPG had just hit his Black Hawk, however the helicopter seemed to be responding to his control movements. Another Black Hawk, *Super Six-Two*, had witnessed the RPG firing, and spoke with Durant to make sure he was safe. A chunk of the tail rotor had been blown off, and the pilot of *Super Six-Two*, Chief Warrant Officer Mike Goffena, recommended that he should return to base – about a four minute flight South-west.

Durant agreed to return to base with Goffena providing escort, but they had barely started a turn, when the rear section of the tail rotor fell off, sending the Black Hawk into a spin. Durant fought desperately to break the spin by turning off one of the engines. Just before he hit the ground, the helicopter levelled and he was able to slow the descent rate enough to pancake the Black Hawk into a few tin huts, this helped to absorb some of the crash inertia. Durant and his co-pilot Ray Frank were the only ones to survive the crash of *Super Six-Four*, however they were both badly injured. Durant grabbed his personnel weapon and began firing on the Somalis, who were trying to surround him. The situation was now critical, the convoy was ordered to secure the crash site of Durant's Black Hawk, but at this stage they hadn't even found Wolcott's crash site.

The convoy was now heading North towards Armed Forces Road. As they drove up the road a number of the soldiers in the convoy saw the wreckage of Wolcott's Black Hawk, however they were unaware that this was their objective. The controlling helicopter had now informed them to turn back towards crash site number two. At this point there was a heated exchange between the JOC and ground commanders, as they had already despatched another convoy from HQ to secure Durant's crash site. The second convoy was made up of cooks, clerks, storeman and just about anyone who could carry a gun.

The command and control network was now a shambles, when orders were issued nobody knew who they were for and, as a result, unnecessary casualties were being taken. At one stage the first convoy passed the wreckage of Wolcott's Black Hawk twice. The second convoy had also run into trouble on the way and were pinned down. Of the 75 Rangers that had started out on foot towards crash site one, 8 were dead, and over half were injured. At the JOC, a sense of despair had developed, wherever the American forces were going the Somalis were waiting. The Somalis seemed to have no value for their lives. They would often attack the American forces in frontal attacks that would leave dozens of them dead or injured, yet they still kept coming.

Over at Wolcott's crash site, Black Hawk, *Super Six-Eight*, piloted by Dan Jollata was hovering near to the Black Hawk crash site with a number of soldiers ready to be inserted to secure the area. Suddenly there was a loud bang. He had taken a direct hit, and was in trouble. Jollata was fully aware of the fact that he had men hanging from the ropes below him, and in a very courageous act, he put his life on the line, until all of the soldiers were safe on the ground. His helicopter was streaming black smoke, due to oil leaking from the engines, yet with amazing flying skills he managed to coax the Black Hawk back to base where he made a safe landing.

At Durant's crash site, the Somalis were gathering again for another attack. Just as they were about to surge forward, Mike Goffena in *Super Six-Two*, flew over the site and dropped in two Delta Force snipers, who had bravely volunteered to go in and protect Durant until the arrival of convoy two. The Delta soldiers, Randy Shughart and Gary Gordan, assured Durant that everything would be fine. As they fought against the Somali gunmen, there was a scream – Gordan had just been killed, leaving just two against the Somalis. One can only imagine the intense fear that these brave men endured. Durant suddenly realized that there was no more shooting from behind the helicopter, which meant that Shughart had also been killed. Durant felt that this was the end. As he lay on the ground, dozens of frenzied Somalis started to clamber over the wreckage of his helicopter towards him. They dragged him down the street beating him and stripping him of all his clothes. Durant was convinced that he would be killed, but to his amazement, a Somali started to protect him from the mob. However this was not out of any kindness or compassion, it was simply the fact that he was worth nothing dead, but alive he could be exchanged for Somali prisoners. As a result Durant ended up in Aideed's hands and he was eventually released in return for the Warlord's Lieutenants.

As for the rest of the operation, the convoys eventually reached their objectives and the American soldiers withdrew back to their base. The operation had been a disaster, with 18 Americans dead and more than 70 badly injured. The Somalis had lost over 500 with more than a thousand injured, yet they had won. The Somalis knew that this action would cause America to withdraw from Operation 'Restore Hope' and they were right. They had inflicted a disaster on the American armed forces, which to this day remains a sensitive subject. Even recently in Kosovo, the subject of Mogadishu raised its ugly head again proving that it is to haunt America for years to come. Although if there is a grain of salvation to be had from the operation, it is for the incredible bravery displayed by both the soldiers and aircrews, along with some of the finest flying the world has ever seen.

CHAPTER 8
BASHER FIVE-TWO
Mike Ryan

To be shot down and captured behind enemy lines is a pilot's worst nightmare. The emotive images of pilots being paraded on Iraqi TV, after being severely beaten, will always be etched in the minds of American pilots serving on operational tours. In the American rescue world, it is usually assumed that if a pilot is not rescued within four hours of being shot down, he will not be rescued at all. America has the best CSAR (Combat Search and Rescue) capability in the world, and if one of its pilots is shot down, everything possible will be done to rescue them.

In June 1995, American Forces carried out a spectacular rescue mission that involved more than 40 aircraft and helicopters. All of this effort was for just one man, Captain Scott W. O'Grady, an F-16C pilot from the 555th ('Triple Nickel') FS/31st Fighter Wing. At the time of his rescue, Capt O'Grady had been taking part in Operation 'Deny Flight'. A UN sanctioned operation to secure peace in war-torn Bosnia, by means of reinforcing an air exclusion zone that had been set up to eliminate the use of air power by the former Yugoslavia.

He had been based at Aviano in Italy, when on the morning of 2 June 1995, both he and his wingman, Capt Bob Wright, were tasked with flying a sortie over Bosanski Petrovac, near the town of Banja Luka in northern Bosnia. They had been given the mission callsigns of *Basher Five-Two* (O'Grady) and *Basher Five-One* (Wright), with a briefing to carry out low-level sweeps over their assigned areas in search of Serbian forces. As the two F-16s carried out their mission, O'Grady's F-16C was targeted by a Bosnian Serb SA-6 SAM, which was located in a Serbian stronghold to the south of Bihac. He was flying directly above a missile battery that had not been detected by NATO. Without any warning from his underfuselage ECM pod, the Serbs locked on to him and launched a missile. With only a few seconds until impact O'Grady received a threat warning, but it was too late for him to take any evasive action and the warhead struck the middle of the aircraft, causing it to split in half. A huge fireball engulfed the F-16 and O'Grady only just managed to eject from the aircraft before it exploded.

His wingman had seen the explosion, but was unable to see if O'Grady had escaped, as the cockpit section of the F-16 was still intact as it entered cloud. Still in shock from what he had just witnessed, Wright called in the hit and marked the position. O'Grady had 'banged out' at an altitude of 26,000 ft, he was still conscious, however he had sustained burn injuries to his face and neck.

There was still a long way to go down until O'Grady would reach the cover of the forests below. He was well aware of the fact that it was still daylight and felt very exposed as he descended towards an open grass-covered area, upon which he was aiming to land. As he drifted towards the clearing, he passed over a main highway and spotted a group of Serbs looking up at him with bemusement. This was not a good situation – the area would soon be crawling with Serbian troops looking for him and these people would be able to spot his landing point. O'Grady hit the ground running. As soon as he landed, he ditched his parachute and ran towards some nearby bushes. Once in cover, he plastered mud and dirt on his hands and face to cover any exposed skin. He knew he was in danger and the sooner he disappeared, the better his chances of survival were. O'Grady was quick to adapt to his situation and got out of the landing area fast, heading for the nearby forests that he knew would provide good cover. Within minutes of his landing, the Serbs were swarming all over the area in a bid to capture him. The Serbs knew that a captured pilot would be of immense political value to them and spared no effort in searching for him.

O'Grady had picked his ground well. The area was pockmarked with caves that had been used in World War II by the partisans in their fight against the Nazis – it would take the Serbs weeks to search each one thoroughly. O'Grady now had a fighting chance, he knew that if he could just keep his nerve and evade the Serbian search teams, he had a good chance of making it. Over the next few days, the Serbs continued to search the area, often coming within feet of him. He stayed concealed during the day and foraged around at night for food and water. Moving around at night was important because the temperatures dropped below freezing, and if he stayed still, he risked hypothermia. To further add to O'Grady's discomfort it rained during the day, making things more difficult for him. The only good thing about the rain was the fact that it gave him something to drink, as he had used up his eight 4oz emergency water packs from his survival kit.

American pilots were issued with excellent survival kits, which included water packs, snack bars, first aid kit, flares, signal mirror, compass, radio batteries and a 9mm pistol with spare ammunition clips. They also wore a survival vest containing an evasion chart, which gave details on Bosnia, along with tips for finding food. The vest also held camouflage paint, signal mirror, compass, a GPS receiver, first aid kit and a PRC-112 survival radio. This device weighed 28oz, and was about the size of a personal stereo. It could operate for up to seven hours on a single battery and was, without doubt, the best piece of kit that the pilots carried, as it enabled them to talk to other aircraft.

O'Grady had already tried to use his survival radio, however due to bad weather the NATO fighters had been grounded for a few days and because of this his attempts to make contact had failed. O'Grady knew that he had to make contact, because at this point nobody knew if he was dead or alive. Back in Aviano and the Pentagon, the planners were desperate to hear something. They knew that he had not been captured because the Serbs would have wasted no time in bragging about it, and they would have certainly paraded him on Serbian national TV for political reasons in an attempt to embarrass NATO.

As the weather cleared over Bosnia NATO aircraft flew constant sorties in an attempt to make contact with O'Grady. Satellite based intelligence was also being used to locate him. O'Grady had to help himself and was well aware of the aircraft flying over him. He decided to take the risk of making contact and located a site on a hill that gave him a high broadcast point, as well as a landing spot for a helicopter. O'Grady began transmission and very soon an F-18 Hornet confirmed to Aviano that they were receiving signals from O'Grady's beacon. Although aircraft had reported intermittent transmission signals during the first five days, this was the first real contact from *Basher Five-Two*. At first everyone was ecstatic about the transmissions, however this was quickly moderated to cautious optimism that they were genuine and not a Serbian trick. There was only one way to find out; a huge intelligence net was thrown over the region by the Pentagon and the CIA were tasked with sweeping the area with Satellites in a bid to photograph O'Grady. Other specialist aircraft were brought in to support the operation – these included Signals Intelligence (SIGINT) aircraft and infra-red equipped aircraft that were able to detect body heat.

Early one morning an F-16, flown by Capt Thomas Hanford of the 555th, received direct contact from O'Grady during a search sortie. The transmission was, "I'm alive-help." Hanford confirmed acknowledgement of the signal, and asked O'Grady to identify the unit in Korea that he served with. He responded with the answer, and the signal was authenticated. They now knew that O'Grady, callsign *Basher Five-Two*, was alive.

Within minutes of Aviano receiving the news about O'Grady, a rescue mission was being planned. F-18 Hornets from VMA(AW)-533 were despatched to the search area to establish his exact position on the ground. The first F-18 to arrive on scene was flown by Capt David Ehlert. He made a fast pass over the area to let O'Grady know that they were on to him. Minutes later a second F-18 flown by an old friend of O'Grady's, Capt Will Thomas, overflew the site and made direct radio contact. He obtained accurate coordinates of O'Grady's position and left the area. The American pilots had to be very careful not to give away O'Grady's position, as the Serbs were in the area. They began flying intensive sorties over other areas in an attempt to lure the Serbs away from the real rescue site, as they didn't want to lose anyone else.

O'Grady's position was relayed over to Col Martin Berndt, commander of the 24th Marine Expeditionary Unit aboard the *USS Kearsarge* (a Marine helicopter carrier that was on standby in the Adriatic). The Pentagon had given Berndt permission to execute a rescue mission as soon as possible, using all of the ser-vices and agencies of the US Armed Forces if need be. Berndt called together his officers and men and began briefing them on the rescue mission and how it would be executed. The Marines use a rescue system known as TRAP – Tactical Recovery of Aircraft and Personnel. The main difference between the Air Force's 'Combat SAR' and TRAP is that the Air Force cannot recover aircraft. This is due to their methods of operation, which require the minimum usage of both manpower and aircraft. The Marines, on the other hand, try to recover the aircraft if possible as they are usually operating in out-of-area theatres and additional support may not be possible. A typical TRAP recovery team would comprise:

AIR assets: Two AH-1W Super Cobras, two CH-53E Sea Stallions, four AV-8B Harrier jets for CAP (Combat air patrols), as well as support assets such as AWACs aircraft, EW aircraft and fighters if possible such as F-16s and F-18s.

Ground assets: Security Element (Normally 15 Marines), this force is used to secure the immediate area surrounding the helicopters upon landing. Search Element (Normally 15 Marines), this force is used to find the pilot after landing, as in many cases the pilot may be injured and unable to walk to the helicopter. Also at night it can very difficult to locate personnel without the aid of torches, so a ground sweep is often needed to find them.

After a pilot has ejected from an aircraft behind enemy lines, in addition to injury, he may also be in shock and severely traumatized as a result of the experience. This is a situation that the ground force is equipped to deal with and if necessary they may sedate the pilot for his own safety and protection. A typical TRAP team is well enough equipped to penetrate some 100 miles into enemy territory in order to perform a rescue, be it for a pilot or a soldier. The TRAP team will also rescue non-US personnel such as UN or NATO members. The team is well trained to defend itself from SAM systems as well as enemy ground forces.

The typical TRAP mission profile is carried out at low-level, with the Cobra gunships escorting the CH-53s until they are about ten miles from the target area. At this point the Cobras scout ahead to locate, identify and secure the area. Once the area is secure, they will call in the CH-53s for the pick-up. After completion of this stage of the mission, the Cobras escort them back to the ship via a different extraction route. Waiting offshore is another TRAP team of even greater strength, ready to provide additional support if required. Col Berndt had his TRAP team ready and waiting to go onboard the *Kearsarge*. The team consisted of two AH-1W Super Cobra gunships. The first flown by flight leader Maj Scott 'Mick' Mykleby and co-pilot Capt Ian 'Blondie' Walsh. The second flown by wingman Maj Nick 'Festus' Hall with co-pilot Capt Jim 'Jinx' Jenkins; with two AV-8B Harrier jets and two CH-53 Super Stallions for the pick-up. Providing mission support were a pair of Navy E-A6B Prowlers; a USAF EF-111A jamming aircraft; a brace of Marine Corps F-18C/D Hornets for air-cover and two USAF A-10 Warthog close air support aircraft. This entire force was duplicated in case of an emergency and overall command and control of all air assets was assigned to an AWACs platform. In all there were some 40 aircraft and helicopters in this TRAP package, making it the largest force ever to be used in a rescue mission over Europe.

The armada of aircraft and helicopters were now ready to execute the mission, the first to leave were the TRAP helicopters from the *Kearsarge*. They were forced to orbit the Adriatic for almost an hour, until the rest of the package arrived from Aviano and other aircraft carriers that were supporting the operation. At this time O'Grady was unaware of the imminent rescue attempt, he knew that something was going to be attempted, however he had no idea of what time, or even what day, the rescue was likely to happen.

There had been some inter-service politics over who would carry out the rescue; the USAF had wanted to carry out the pick-up using their MH-53s, in a night time operation, as this was their preferred time of mission execution. There were good sound reasons for a night extraction. This was due to the fact that the Serbs possessed very little night vision equipment and would therefore find it extremely difficult to shoot down rescue helicopters, as they would be unable to see them. At night the sound of an MH-53 carries for miles, so although they can be heard at great distances, due to the distinctive sound of their rotor blades, it is very hard to actually pick them out in the sky, especially if the weather is poor. As much as the USAFs argument was strong, the Pentagon wanted O'Grady back as soon as possible. The decision to go with the Marines, was mainly down to the fact that their TRAP rescue could be attempted almost twenty-four hours before the USAF rescue would be possible. The Pentagon accepted that a daylight rescue was far more risky, however the Marines argued the fact that the longer O'Grady was in Bosnia, the greater the risk of him being captured by the Serbs. As a result of this argument, the mission went to the Marines.

From O'Grady's point of view, he didn't care who carried out the rescue. After spending six days evading enemy capture and living off the land in freezing conditions, he just wanted to go home. The Cavalry were now well on their way to rescuing O'Grady. As they crossed Serbian territory, they dropped down to 200ft for their short 50-minute flight to O'Grady's marked position. As they neared his position, they radioed him for final directions and an authenticity check. He gave them directions as to his position on the hill and as the helicopters neared his rough location they asked him to 'pop' smoke. O'Grady fired a red smoke grenade, however due to the strong wind it quickly dissipated. A Cobra gunship appeared over O'Grady for a short moment to drop a yellow smoke grenade, this was done to mark the spot for the CH-53s which were following close behind the scout Cobras. The first CH-53 to arrive was flown by Maj William Tarbutton, as it crossed a nearby pine fence it flared and landed, near to the edge of the site. As soon as the helicopter had come to rest, the rear ramp lowered and twenty Marines ran out of the back to secure the immediate area. The two Cobras combed the nearby forest looking for any signs of Serbian forces – so far everything was going as planned. The second CH-53 was flown by Capt Paul Fortunato and his co-pilot Capt James Wright, also on board was Col Berndt. It had been orbiting nearby and started to make its approach towards O'Grady. As it commenced its landing it hit a barbed wire fence, thankfully there was no damage to the helicopter. As they landed they saw O'Grady running towards the helicopter with his 9mm pistol in hand – he was wearing an orange survival hat for identification. It was a great moment for everyone onboard to see him alive and well after being through such an ordeal. The crew opened the side door of the CH-53 to let O'Grady onboard and the Marines quickly returned to the helicopter. Once onboard, the two helicopters lifted into the air and turned for base. O'Grady was given food and water and thermal blankets to help restore his body heat – after living for 6 days in freezing conditions his body temperature had dropped dramatically. The entire ground rescue had taken less than nine minutes and the crews had performed extremely well, however they were not out of the woods yet. President Clinton had been following the rescue and asked to be informed as soon as O'Grady was safe. The Marines sent the President a simple message: 'Got him'.

On the way in there had been no problems with the Serbian SAM systems, however on the way out things were going to be different. On the way in they had travelled at around 120mph, on the way out they sped along at 170mph and for the first thirty miles there were no problems. As they entered a small valley all hell broke loose, three shoulder launched SA-7 SAMS were fired at them, however all missed. Just as they cleared this hurdle, they encountered AAA systems and small arms fire. The CH-53s were taking multiple hits, with many rounds piercing the cabin – although nobody had yet been injured from the incoming rounds. The pilots of the helicopters banked hard to port, then hard to starboard in an attempt to dodge the AAA. One of the pilots later described the AAA as being "like huge orange base-balls, passing over us". The helicopters had not encountered any of this on the way in, due in part to the heavy fog that had cov-ered most of the Bosnian countryside earlier that morning. The CH-53s and Cobras were now on an E-ticket ride, many of them openly admitted that this flight had been the most frightening of their lives. One minute the helicopters were on the deck, the next soaring to clear power lines that criss-crossed the valleys. As the helicopters violently manoeuvred along the valley floors, they fired off burning decoy flares to try and deflect the incoming SAMs and this technique proved successful as no helicopters were hit. The fog provided some degree of protection from the AAA as the Serbian systems only had optical sights. If they couldn't see them, they couldn't shoot them and at last they were finally clear – everybody gave a sigh of relief. As for Capt O'Grady he looked relieved to be out of it. He had already been through one nightmare and now he had survived another.

As they approached the *USS Kearsarge*, just about everybody had turned out on deck to greet O'Grady and his rescuers. This was a very proud moment for the American armed forces, as they had pulled off a spectacular rescue without any losses. A clear message went out to all of America's pilots – that if they ever found themselves in the same circumstances as Capt Scott O'Grady they knew that everything possible would be done to get them back. At home Capt O'Grady received a hero's welcome for the courage that he displayed during his six-day ordeal. His rescuers were also treated as heroes, with many of them receiving medals in recognition of their courage for what had been an extremely difficult mission. Their flying skills were also praised throughout the services, as a good example of how to perform and execute a rescue mission.

CHAPTER 9
SEARCHING FOR EBRO 33
Mike McKinney

Operation 'Deliberate Force' was prompted by the shelling of a market in downtown Sarajevo on 28 August, 1995. This cowardly attack killed 38 people and was carried out by Bosnian Serb Army (BSA) forces sitting high in the hills surrounding Sarajevo. They relentlessly used mortars and snipers to harass the Muslims living in the city. For more than a year, Western journalists covered every attack in detail and despite the best efforts of politicians, the violence continued. Public reaction in the West was severe in calling for military action against the BSA. Finally, the leaders of the concerned Western nations decided to retaliate with air power. The plan had been laid out many months prior to the start. NATO air forces would strike at the BSA's war-making capability. Targets included fielded forces, troop barracks, command and control facilities and ammunition depots. This was not the first use of NATO air power in the region. In 1994, several strikes were carried out against airfields and surface-to-air missile (SAM) batteries throughout the country. On 2 June 1995, a US F-16 fighter jet was shot down by a Bosnian Serb SA-6 battery. The NATO leaders realized that the possibility of another such incident could definitely occur. They were willing to take that risk and at 0212 hours on 30 August, the first bomb reached its target.

At 1716 hours, *Ebro 33*, a French Air Force Mirage 2000K was struck by an infrared SAM, presumably an SA-16 Gimlet.

The crew ejected safely and landed about 20 miles south-east of Palé, the Bosnian Serb capital. 'Deliberate Force' was less than 24 hours old and the first aircraft had been lost. Although two good chutes were seen, efforts to reach the crew by radio proved hopeless. As the night went on, not one word was heard about *Ebro 33*. It was felt that the Serbs would surely announce their capture to the world. The NATO staff deduced that the crew must be evading, unable to talk due to the presence of Serb search parties. Efforts intensified to locate *Ebro 33*. German Air Force Tornado reconnaissance fighters were tasked to take detailed photos of the area. As the photo interpreters scanned the photos over the next couple of days, images began to emerge. It appeared that the search and rescue (SAR) letter of the day was laid out in a field using tree limbs. In another photo, a delta symbol with 'EB3' spelled out next to it could be seen drawn on a dirt road. At least that is vaguely what these photos appeared to show. The delta symbol could represent the Mirage fighter with its delta wing shape. And while the letters did not necessarily spell out the correct callsign, it could be all the crew could get out. Or they could be nothing at all. Interpreting vague signs from aerial photos is more of an art than a science, but the people that do this job are very skilled. Since the Serbs still had not acknowledged their capture and nothing had been heard on the radio, it was felt that *Ebro 33* was still evading.

During the attacks, the CSAR coverage was provided by MH-53J Pave Lows from the 20th and 21st Special Operations Squadrons. Typically, they would launch from Brindisi, an Italian Air Base in the heel of Italy, and orbit just off the coast of Bosnia until the air strikes were over. Four helicopters would make up the CSAR package. Two Pave Lows were designated the primary recovery flight while the other two would remain off the coast. These last two carried a robust Special Forces (SF) ground team in the back to provide a rescue force for the first two Pave Lows. Unlike an ejection seat aircraft, when a helicopter is shot down, the scene can be sheer chaos. Having to actually go in and pull the injured and dead out of a downed helicopter can take hours. The SF team was there to do just that, get everyone out and secure the area while the rescue takes place. From the beginning of the *Ebro 33* incident, the staff of Joint Special Operations Task Force 2 (JSOTF2) watched the situation closely. JSOTF2 was the term for the combined special operations units located at Brindisi. Included in this mix were AC-130H gunships, HC-130P Combat Shadow tankers, Navy SEALs, and Army Special Forces. They knew that if *Ebro 33* were spotted, their aircraft would get the call to conduct the rescue. Although on the morning of 6 September, this was almost not the case. During the early morning hours, there were small indications that *Ebro 33* might be trying to signal again. Radio beacons were briefly heard. The decision was made to launch an armed reconnaissance of the area by helicopter. JSOTF2 planners knew that it would by daylight by the time the Pave Lows reached the Bosnian coastline. In a country like Bosnia, the last thing a Pave Low crew wants to do is fly in the daytime. Every house had some kind of weapon, and the occupants were not afraid to use it. It would be suicide. The JSOTF2 staff refused the request instead saying that a mission could be launched that evening. Also waiting and watching were Navy HH-60 helicopters stationed aboard the aircraft carrier, *USS George Washington*. They were sitting just off the coast and could conduct the mission before daybreak. NATO leaders gave the HH-60s the go for the rescue attempt.

Two HH-60s launched from the *Washington* and proceeded

northbound into Bosnia. Just a few miles inside the coastline, they encountered thick fog. Weaving around the fog, the helicopters pressed on. Soon the fog became too thick for the mission to continue and they had to turn around. On the way outbound, small arms fire erupted and one of the helicopters was slightly damaged but made it safely back to the carrier. The Navy helicopters were just not the correct choice for this mission. Although they had some CSAR training, they were not as highly trained for the mission as the Pave Low crews. They also lacked the defensive systems and sophisticated avionics of the Pave Lows, who were perfectly suited for the threats and the weather. Back in Brindisi, the JSOTF2 staff watched the action and boiled inside. Earlier in the year, nearly the same thing happened when a US Marine rescue force rescued Capt Scott O'Grady. The Pave Lows were also initially tasked with that mission, but again declined in order to wait for nightfall. Sitting just off the coast were the Marines and they were given the mission. Although the mission was supposed to happen during the remainder of the night, by the time the Marines reached O'Grady, the sun was high on the horizon. The Pave Low crews felt that because of their insistence on conducting all operations at night, they were once again going to lose a piece of the action. During the day, the NATO air staff decided that because of the threat and terrain, only the Pave Lows would conduct any future rescue attempts. This energized the JSOTF2 staff and they prepared for follow-on taskings.

Another attempt was scheduled for the night of 7 September. Routing in and out of the country was meticulously scrutinized using computer-based flight planning systems. In the on-going conflict in Bosnia, nearly everyone had a gun. The worst part was that they were more than willing to shoot at anything, no one was considered friendly. For the Pave Lows, the best chance for survival was to plan around every village and troop concentration. Covering the helicopters would be an AC-130H, in addition to A-10 and F/A-18D fighters. The crews chosen for the mission show the diversity of the operation. Flight lead for the Pave Lows was Capt Mark Harmon from the 21st SOS. His co-pilot was Capt Todd Lancaster from the 20th SOS. In the second Pave Low was Capt Mike Moncrief from the 20th and Capt Rob McCreadie from the 21st. They were given the callsigns *Knife 44* and *47* respectively. In addition to their standard load of tow pararescuemen (PJ) and one combat controller, each helicopter would carry a French Commando. His job was to act as interpreter and would deploy with the team if needed. Each Pave Low was armed with two GAU-2 7.62mm miniguns and one GAU-18 .50 calibre machine gun. The miniguns can fire at rates of 2000-4000 rounds per minute but have a fairly small bullet. On the other hand the .50 cal. delivers quite a punch and is mounted on the aft ramp to give the gunner a better field of fire. On the hour-long flight across the Adriatic, each gunner tested his weapon to make sure it would work properly if needed. The crews also checked the defensive avionics and chaff and flare systems. By this point in the conflict, the Serbs were known and well respected for their prowess with SAMs. The one final piece of equipment checked out was the terrain-following/ terrain-avoidance (TF/TA) radar. If the fog developed like it had for the HH-60s the night before, the TF/TA radar was the only means of conducting the mission safely. The Pave Low was the only helicopter in the world capable of operating as low as 100 feet above the ground in zero visibility.

Knife 44 flight crossed the coastline north-west of the town of Bacina. Working their way northward they stayed well to the west of Mostar, a large city in the Neretva River valley. They dashed across the valley and headed towards the area where *Ebro 33* was thought to be located. Everything was going well, no anti-aircraft fire had been seen and very few inhabitants. As they got into the search area the fog started to develop once again. Although the Pave Lows can fly in the fog, a visual search is impossible. As the fog thickened the search was aborted and the flight headed home. Unfortunately, they only searched for about a quarter of the planned time. On the way out of the country, the flight took small arms fire about 20 miles from the coast. One bullet hole was found in a main rotor of *Knife 47* after the mission. That night a review of the video taken by the orbiting AC-130H showed what appeared to be two figures walking out of the trees toward an open field. This was exactly the area searched by the helicopters but occurred after they left. This led many to believe that these figures were *Ebro 33* prompting a second mission. The same crews were scheduled for the mission and were told to get plenty of rest.

The third attempt to locate *Ebro 33* was launched on 7 September 1995. Many of the crewmembers felt uncomfortable about going back into Bosnia for the second time. They were sure that they would take fire but were determined to get the mission done. The weather was much better this night and the moon was bright. This also meant that the BSA gunners could see the Pave Lows as well. *Knife 44* searched the primary area while *Knife 47* stayed back to provide fire support if needed. About half of the search was complete when *Knife 47* took small arms fire. At about the same time, *Knife 44* came under heavy attack while still in the search area. It appeared that a trap had been set for the helicopters. It was time to get out. As the helicopters started out of the search area, the gunfire lit up the sky. *Knife 44* took several hits, the helicopter shuddered and warning lights flashed. One round penetrated the bottom of the helicopter, hit a beam in the ceiling, then split into pieces. One piece hit flight engineer SSgt Dennis Turner in the knee. Another struck the left-side gunner, SSgt Randy Rutledge. Turner yelled out "I'm hit!" but maintained his position behind his minigun in the right door. A PJ rushed forward to check out the injuries. Both Turner and Rutledge were bleeding profusely and the PJ applied bandages to try and control it. The flight still had a long way to go before safety. Back in the JSOTF2 compound, the first word of the trouble came via a relay from the orbiting AC-130. The mood quickly darkened. The gunners returned fire, several times quite accurately. One gunner could clearly see his .50 cal. rounds impact a man as he fired his AK-47 at the helicopters. On the gunship video, tracers can be seen coming from a small building. The helicopters appear streaming tracers right back into the house. The fire from the house stops. Overhead the gunship and fighters attack numerous targets; a fully-fledged battle has ensued. Just prior to the coast, the helicopters pop out of the mountains into a wide-open valley. Large anti-aircraft artillery (AAA) pieces open up on the flight. Airburst rounds detonate in the night sky and impact on the hillsides. Just as the tracers appear to be triangulating on the helicopters, they hop over a ridge to safety. The muzzle flashes accidentally set off the automatic flare dispenser in one Pave Low – lighting up the sky even more. From the other Pave Low, it briefly appears as if the helicopter has exploded. Finally the helicopters make it to the safety of the Adriatic, but they still have a one-hour flight home. The durability of the Pave Low pays off, the flight lands at Brindisi, greeted by waiting medical personnel. Rutledge and Turner are rushed onto a waiting MC-130 and taken to Naples for surgery to remove the fragments. Each helicopter took hits that night. Several bullet holes are found in the main rotor blades, fuselage and fuel tank sponsons. Fortunately no major damage or injuries occur. The search for *Ebro 33* comes to an end as the risks are just too high to be justified. Without further concrete evidence that they are still evading, no missions will be launched.

Efforts to locate *Ebro 33* continue until 28 September, when French authorities tell NATO leaders they believe the crew is in the custody of the Serbs. Finally, on 13 December, *Ebro 33* was released in good health. They were captured almost immediately after landing in their parachutes. The source of the signals on the ground and the radio beacons still remain a mystery. Could this have been a trap set by the BSA to shoot down the helicopters? The truth will probably never be known. The search for *Ebro 33* marks the first time Pave Low gunners fired shots in anger. For their heroic efforts, the crews of *Knife 44* and *47* were awarded the Cheney Award. This award is given for an act of valour, extreme fortitude, or self-sacrifice in a humanitarian interest performed in connection with an Air Force aircraft. SSgts. Turner and Rutledge each receive the Purple Heart, a first for Pave Low aircrew. This mission highlights the importance of operating at night. Had *Knife 44* flight attempted these missions in the day, they most certainly could have ended up in the same circumstances as *Ebro 33*. Pave Low crews stuck to their tactics in regards to the O'Grady mission and lost the glory. Unfortunate as that may be, the opposite could just as very easily have occurred. With every combat situation comes a percentage of luck. The crews of *Knife 44* and *47* definitely had a high percentage of luck on those two nights.

CHAPTER 10
THE LAST AIR WAR OF THE MILLENNIUM
Mike McKinney

Contrary to popular belief, Operation 'Allied Force' was not planned overnight. The wheels had been set in motion almost a year before the first bombs fell on Serbia. Unit planners assembled a powerful air campaign designed to make the Serbian leadership think long and hard about the importance of Kosovo. Strategic targets would be attacked on the first night in the same fashion as the start of 'Desert Storm' – designed to cripple the infrastructure of the nation. As time went by the situation changed and the planners adapted by changing the target sets. Political pressures made it impossible to continue on the original path, and the air campaign was reduced to a slow, reactionary response in an effort to bring Slobodan Milosevic back to the bargaining table. One aspect that overshadowed the entire plan was the very capable Serbian air defence system. Trained during the Cold War to fight against NATO, the air defence operators of the former Yugoslavia were very skilled and resourceful. They had received some of the best training and equipment the Soviets could offer. In June 1995, they showcased these skills by downing Capt Scott O'Grady's F-16 over Bosnia with an SA-6 missile. Now, many of these same air defence operators were waiting to do exactly what they had trained for years ago; defending their homeland from NATO attackers. One advantage for NATO pilots was that since the collapse of the Eastern-bloc, the Serbs were unable to acquire any of the advanced surface-to-air missiles (SAM) being produced by the Russians. The majority of their inventory included 1960s-era SA-3 Goa and SA-6 Gainful missiles. On the night of 27 March 1999, the Serbs proved once again that it's not always the age of the equipment, but the skill of the operator, that gets results.

Four days into the bombing campaign, the atmosphere at the Joint Special Operations Task Force- Noble Anvil (JSOTF-NA) compound in Brindisi, Italy was beginning to calm down. The air war could be watched in the command centre on a projected display of aircraft and threat activity. During the opening nights, the scene resembled a championship football game, anyone who had the time crowded into the room to watch the action unfold. By now, there remained only a handful of die-hard watchers, but the scene would quickly change. The night began just like the previous nights. Low clouds obscured many of the targets for the fighter packages. Due to political restraints, all aircraft were limited in the selection of their ingress and egress routes. The standard flow was from the south, through either Macedonian or Albanian airspace, then egressing to the north over Croatia or Hungary. What most of the participants in the air campaign did not know this night was that the stealth aircraft were still on schedule for their missions. Because of their GPS-guided munitions, the stealth aircraft were not as affected by the weather. For three previous nights, the stealth aircraft operated with little resistance. While the details of the downing remain classified, what is known is that on the night of 27 March, several SAMs were launched at *Vega 31*, an F-117 Nighthawk, as it neared its target. For reasons unknown, the F-117 went out of control and the pilot was forced to eject. This seemed to catch much of the Allied air package by surprise. The thought of an aircraft being shot down was always a possibility but not an F-117. Stealth aircraft had flown hundreds of combat hours in Panama and Iraq without suffering as much as a scratch. It can be said that a feeling of complacency surrounded stealth operations due to this success. Luckily, the pilot of *Vega 31* did not suffer from this complacency and was well prepared for possible eventualities over the next several hours. The identity of the pilot remains classified therefore he will be referred to using his callsign. As he floated down in his parachute, *Vega 31* was already thinking ahead. He immediately broke out his survival radio and began trying to contact any aircraft around him. This mayday call was picked up by several aircraft and echoed throughout the Combined Air Operations Centre (CAOC) in Vincenza, Italy. Thus began a long night of frustration and ultimately elation.

Sitting on alert in Tuzla, Bosnia was a combined flight of 20th, 21st and 55th SOS helicopter crews. Leading the flight was Capt Jim Cardoso and his co-pilot Capt John Glass in *Moccasin 60*, an MH-53M Pave Low IV of the 20th SOS. Second in the flight was *Moccasin 61*, an MH-53J Pave Low IIIE flown by Capt Shawn Cameron and Capt Mark Daley from the 21st SOS. Finally, was *Gator 01*, an MH-60G Pavehawk of the 55th SOS flown by Capt Chad Frank and Capt Matt Glover. The makeup of this flight was not as confusing as it appears; it was the standard formation adopted by the Joint Special Operations Task Force 2 (JSOTF2) planning staff. For years the responsibility for CSAR in the theatre fell on the shoulders of the 21st SOS 'Dust Devils', stationed at RAF Mildenhall, in the United Kingdom. Since 1993, the 21st had maintained a constant presence by operating a detachment at Brindisi; an Italian Air Force Base located in the 'heel' of Italy. The 'Green Hornets' of the 20th SOS augmented the 21st through the years, giving the smaller squadron a much-needed break from the relentless deployment schedule. As the plan for Allied Force developed it became clear that more helicopters would be needed to conduct both CSAR and special operations missions simultaneously. The 20th and 55th were alerted and deployed to the theatre with little notice, arriving just a few days prior to the start of operations. For the men of the 55th SOS, 'Nighthawks', Allied Force represented the first and last time the unit would operate in the theatre. The squadron was scheduled for deactivation that very summer, giving them one last moment of glory.

When word of *Vega 31's* downing reached Tuzla, the crews immediately assembled in the makeshift operations centre and began gathering information. The location of *Vega 31* was unknown. His target was known but where he had actually come down remained elusive. One source placed him in downtown Belgrade, not a good option for the CSAR flight. Another placed him fairly close to the target, but this turned out to be a report of the crash site itself. Throughout the night, *Vega 31's* location became the priority of every aircraft involved in the search. The initial CSAR plan called for a solid survivor location within one mile before committing the helicopters. What no one wanted was to have to orbit inside Serbia searching for a survivor. If this happened, the loss of helicopters and men would most certainly occur. All of the information eventually led to one location in the northern region of Serbia, near the Croatian border. This seemed logical since *Vega 31's* flight path would have taken him right over this area. As with every CSAR, time is the critical factor. The longer the survivor stays on the ground, the greater the chance he will be picked up by enemy forces. With *Vega 31*, time was wasting away quickly. On CNN, the world watched Serbian military personnel and civilians examining the still burning wreckage of the F-117. Meanwhile, *Vega 31* was still on the ground, hiding in a drainage ditch several miles away. He would remain there for several more hours before being rescued.

The sense of urgency to do simply anything increased by the minute. Using the northern coordinates for *Vega 31's* location, the plan was set in motion to rendezvous with the supporting A-10 rescue escort (RESCORT) aircraft and press in for the pickup. The location was perfect, close to the Croatian border and far away from any air defence units. However, a mistake made somewhere in the decision chain resulted in more confusion. From Aviano AB in Italy, the A-10s passed on their time of arrival at the rendezvous point. In the theatre the difference between local time and Zulu time, the common time reference used in aviation, was only one hour. During the passing of information the rendezvous time was mistaken for local time instead of Zulu time. This made it appear that the A-10s would arrive much earlier than expected. The helicopters quickly launched from Tuzla thinking that their RESCORT would arrive shortly. Cardoso led the flight to the north into Croatia to a point just outside the Serbian border. On the ground, *Vega 31* was quite sure of his location and passed the coordinates to the orbiting command and control aircraft. Ironically, his coordinates fell on deaf ears. Thinking that he was shaken from the ejection and ensuing evasion, *Vega 31's* own information fell to the bottom of the list of sources. This may have been true for many aviators but once again, *Vega 31* was on top of his game and correct with his location. As the helicopters proceeded to the north, the time mistake became apparent; the A-10s were nowhere near. To conserve fuel, Cardoso landed the flight in a large field and waited for the A-10s to arrive. In another twist of fate, Cardoso's

Satellite Communications (SATCOM) radio was not working, which was his main connection to the command staff in Vincenza. The other helicopters had operative SATCOMs but almost on cue, they too stopped receiving any signals once the flight crossed into Croatia. *Moccasin 60* flight was sitting in a Croatian field unable to communicate to anyone. Everyone in the flight was nervous, what started out as the greatest moment of their lives was quickly turning into a nightmare. And to top it all off, *Vega 31's* actual position was much farther to the south than the flight realized.

As *Vega 31* transmitted over his survival radio, intelligence assets narrowed down his location. Finally, the realization was made that *Vega 31* was right where he thought he was, about 20 miles north-west of Belgrade. When he ejected, *Vega 31* was still several thousand feet in the air and the wind had carried him about 10 miles from where his stricken Nighthawk came down. This was fortunate for him since the Serbs were desperately trying to find him. The Serbs knew that capturing an Allied pilot would send shock waves through the coalition, and the thought of having a stealth pilot was the icing on the cake. *Vega 31* was their ace-in-the-hole and they knew he was out there somewhere. In a near miraculous moment, Cardoso overheard the A-10s talking to *Vega 31* on his survival radio. When Cardoso got the new coordinates for *Vega 31* and plotted them on his map, he realized that the flight would have to air refuel to complete the mission. *Moccasin 61* blindly broadcast the flight's intentions over their SATCOM radio in hopes that someone would hear them. The A-10s were now in the area and ready to go but were put on hold. In another act of confusion, the idea of the helicopters refuelling put an unnecessary pause on the operation. To the rest of the Combat Air Forces (CAF), air refuelling means departing the area of operations for orbiting tanker aircraft. This process is done far away from the battle area and can take several hours depending on the distance to the tanker orbits. However, in helicopter air refuelling the tanker aircraft simply rendezvous with the helicopters along the route of flight. The air refuelling is accomplished without a time delay like the CAF model. Unfortunately, this fact was unknown to many and the mission was unnecessarily postponed until the helicopters refuelled. *Moccasin 60* flight took off, headed to the south, met up with an MC-130P Combat Shadow, and finished refuelling in about 30 minutes. Again because of the confusion over air refuelling, the Combat Search and Rescue Task Force (CSARTF) was also sent to awaiting tanker aircraft, a process that lasted nearly two hours.

After holding near the border for over two hours, *Moccasin 60* flight was finally given the final approval to cross the border and proceed with the mission. The A-10s pressed ahead to orbit *Vega 31's* position, check for enemy forces, and make sure *Vega 31* was the correct person. The last step is very important since more than once, CSAR helicopters have fallen into traps set by enemy troops using captured radios. The weather was typical for the region; low clouds obscured everything below the A-10s. Also, the moon had already set, making it a very dark night. The weather was actually beneficial to the helicopters. Helicopter pilots are more comfortable flying in bad weather and it helps mask the aircraft from threats. Flying at slower speeds also lessens the chance of hitting the ground. The only problem in this situation is that the A-10s could not provide cover fire for the helicopters should the need arise. They would have to rely on their own .50 calibre machine guns and 7.62mm miniguns for protection. As the flight crossed the Serbian border, it seemed as if all the visibility had disappeared. The weather and the land-scape of a nation at war combined to make the world much darker to Cardoso and the other members of his flight. In *Moccasin 61*, Mark Daley was trying to navigate using visual references. He located a fairly large city on the map that he felt sure was nearby but just could not see it anywhere. Then one of the gunners called out a town directly below the helicopter. The darkness completely masked the city until directly 100 feet overhead. Luckily, the Pave Low is suited for this eventuality. With a Forward-Looking Infrared (FLIR) system, and a Terrain-Following/ Terrain-Avoidance (TF/TA) radar in the nose, the Pave Low can operate in conditions other helicopters cannot. Coupled to these systems are two pilots and three scanners searching the landscape with Night Vision Goggles (NVG), nervously looking for enemy fire, terrain, powerlines, and towers. This paid off several miles inside the border as a set of wires suddenly came into view just in front of Cardoso's heli-copter. Flying less than 100 feet above the ground, the flight popped up ever so briefly to clear the wires. This near disaster caused Cardoso to gain a little more altitude – no one wants to get killed by the ground.

Overhead, the A-10s had done their job. Although they could not see *Vega 31* because of the weather, they successfully located his position and authenticated his identity. For the helicopters, the flight to *Vega 31's* location was relatively easy. The hard part remained in finding him quickly and getting back out of Serbia. In a scene out of World War II, as *Moccasin 60* flight approached *Vega 31*, searchlights shot up into the night sky, try-ing to locate the helicopters. The primary plan called for *Gator 01* to make the pickup. The MH-60G could fit into smaller land-ing zones (LZ) and manoeuvre quicker than the larger MH-53s.

If all went well, *Gator 01* would swoop in, recover *Vega 31*, and depart the LZ in less than a minute while the MH-53s remained overhead for fire support if needed. But first, they had to find him. Even with all the sophisticated systems on the helicopters, the mission comes down to visually acquiring the survivor. This is the aviation equivalent to finding a needle in a haystack. Luckily, *Vega 31* was in fairly open, agricultural terrain with a great chance of being seen. *Vega 31* reported that he could hear the approaching helicopters but could not see them. Cardoso requested that *Vega 31* light off one of his survival flares to help locate him. Suddenly, the once dark landscape glowed brilliantly for miles as *Vega 31's* flare lit up the sky. The helicopters immediately called for him to extinguish the flare as the intensity was blinding on NVGs. Several vehicles could be seen parked by the roadside within a mile of *Vega's* position. They all had their headlights on – this was quite probably a search party. To *Gator 01* the flare seemed almost directly below the helicopter. Franks pulled back hard on the cyclic stick to slow the Pavehawk down and attempt to make it into the LZ. The helicopter came to a hover and Franks moved over towards *Vega 31's* position. *Vega 31* jumped from his hiding place, stopped just outside the rotor disk of the Pavehawk and asked over the radio if he could enter the helicopter. While this seems unorthodox in combat, it is standard practice to get permission before coming under the rotor disk of a helicopter. This shows just another example of the coolness of *Vega 31*. Obviously, he was given permission and was met just outside the helicopter by a Pararescueman. The two quickly jumped on board and *Gator 01* leaped out of the LZ. It had been nearly five and a half hours since takeoff but they were on the ground less than forty seconds.

Cardoso looked at the map and decided to make a straight

dash for the border. They would be back in Tuzla in about 45 minutes. Thankfully the egress was as uneventful as the ingress and the flight landed at Tuzla nearly eight hours after takeoff. The first combat rescue since 'Desert Storm' had gone off without a hitch and the coalition was saved a huge embarrassment. *Vega 31* was met by medical and intelligence officers and quickly loaded into a waiting MC-130P for a quick flight to Aviano. Although the mission was a success, it highlighted some coordination problems within the plan. It also gave away the details of the plan to the Serbs, a factor that would come into play during the next mission. The Serbs knew that the helicopters would come from Tuzla and beefed up their air defence assets along the border with Bosnia. On 2 May, this would nearly spell disaster for the crews of *Skat 11* flight.

Hammer 34, an F-16CG Fighting Falcon had just come off his target near Novi Sad when an SAM detonated nearby. Although his jet was mortally wounded, it was still flyable and *Hammer 34* glided towards the Bosnian border. Realizing that he would not make it, *Hammer 34* started getting himself and the aircraft around him ready for his rescue. Again in Tuzla, sat a flight of helicopters waiting for the word. This time both Pave Lows belonged to the 20th SOS. In *Skat 11* were Capt Kent Landreth and Lt Tom Palenske. Lt Tom Lang and Lt Dan Nielsen piloted *Skat 12*. The third member of the flight was *Skat 14*, an MH-60G flown by Capt Bill Denehan and Capt Tom Kunkel. The plan remained the same as on the *Vega 31* rescue, but this time things seemed to be going smoother. Since the *Vega 31* mission, the problems that were encountered were debriefed and critiqued among all the players. Changes were made to hopefully smooth out any future missions. *Hammer 34's* wingman was still in the air and once he ejected, his wingman remained overhead for protection. The wingman did not actually see where *Hammer 34* landed, meaning that his exact position was still uncertain. When word of the shootdown reached Tuzla, the greatest concern was the time of day. The sun would be rising in just a few hours and everyone knew that any delays would mean having to attempt the rescue during the early morning hours – a very bad option. Quickly, they went to work analyzing every scrap of information as it came in. *Hammer 34's* general location was known and the pilots gathered around a large map of the theatre to determine the best course of action. The Special Forces team broke out more detailed maps and analyzed the terrain. If *Hammer 34* were injured, the team might have to deploy and search for him on the ground. *Hammer 34's* wingman radioed back that he felt he had a good location. He too knew that the sun would be up in a couple of hours and the time to act was shrinking.

The decision was made to launch the helicopters without the A-10 RESCORT aircraft in the area. This was a bold move because the A-10s provide a tremendous capability in firepower. If they waited and the mission pushed on into the day, even the A-10's firepower might not help *Skat 11* flight. The protection of darkness outweighed the need for RESCORT. *Skat 11* flight departed and headed west toward the border. However, two important factors were going against *Skat 11* flight on this night. First, unlike the *Vega 31* mission, the weather was crystal clear and the moon was nearly full. This meant that Serbian forces would have an easy time spotting the flight, even without night vision devices. Second, the NATO forces weren't the only ones that debriefed and critiqued the *Vega 31* mission. The Serbs made some changes of their own, which *Skat 11* flight was about to brutally find out. Even before the helicopters crossed the border SAMs engaged the flight. In the cockpits, the launches appeared as two small dots of light slowly rising from the ground. Palenske, not knowing the dots were SAMs, commented that the fighters must be "bombing the hell out of the Serbs". Seconds later, the startling revelation was made that these dots were SAMs, and they were headed right towards the flight. Landreth dove for the ground, trying to hide behind any terrain available. The flight followed his lead. Time stood still as everyone locked their eyes on the missiles. In mere seconds, the SAMs flew overhead, missing by less than 200 feet. The night had just begun and they had already had the scare of their lives.

As *Skat 11* flight pressed further into Serbia, anti-aircraft fire dotted the skies in vain attempts to hit the helicopters. A SAM battery engaged the flight a second time, this one splitting the formation. Everyone was tense but no one thought of turning back. The crews could see for miles, and the moon was so bright this night that it resembled the sun. When flying in enemy territory under conditions like these, they felt incredibly exposed – as if everyone knew of their presence and were watching their every move. Landreth manoeuvred the flight around what little terrain he could find, trying desperately to hide the formation. Finally, the flight arrived at the set of coordinates passed to them before takeoff. There was no sign of *Hammer 34*. They immediately began a hasty search of the area, looking for any sign from the downed pilot. *Hammer 34's* wingman finally realized that the location was much further to the east, towards Belgrade. After about seven minutes of searching, the flight received the new set of coordinates and headed out. The A-10 Sandy aircraft finally arrived on station and took over the job of protecting *Hammer 34*. Now all everyone could do was wait for the helicopters to arrive. Inside *Skat 11*, Landreth could see that Serbian air defences were quiet. They obviously knew the rescue was happening, but the Serbs were afraid to turn on their radars for fear of losing them to NATO fighters. This tended to be the general trend of the war. On the ground *Hammer 34* could hear voices and dogs in the distance, the Serbs were also searching for him. It was just a matter of time until someone found him.

As the helicopters approached *Hammer 34's* position they were guided in the last few miles by the A-10s overhead. In similar fashion to the *Vega 31* rescue, Denehan and Kunkel swooped in right next to *Hammer 34*. As he was getting into the Pavehawk shots could be heard in the distance. In less than 30 seconds, the Pavehawk was airborne again and heading toward safety. The glow of the rising sun could be seen in the east and Landreth was very concerned about the egress routing. He definitely did not want to go back out the same way they had just come. In the daylight they would have been sitting ducks. The decision was made to fly as straight and as fast as possible to Tuzla. Not far from the landing zone, *Skat 14* came under fire from someone in a small building. SSgt Rich Kelley, the flight engineer opened fire from the right window with his minigun. His return fire was effective and the enemy fire ceased. The Pavehawk had been hit in several places but luckily nothing was seriously damaged. *Skat 11* flight crossed back into Bosnia with the sun chasing them. By the time they landed at Tuzla, the morning had begun. *Hammer 34* was again whisked away aboard a waiting MC-130 and flown to Aviano for debrief. The second and final rescue of the campaign ended successfully.

Operation 'Allied Force' lasted 78 days. Despite absurd claims made by the Serbian government, only two NATO manned aircraft were destroyed by enemy fire. There were several other close calls but they can be counted on one hand. In the end the Serbian air defence network failed to show up for the fight. They had the equipment and capability to put up a valiant defence yet rightly decided against it. Whether this was the official strategy or the choice of individual air defence commanders may never be known. For the men and women of 'Task Force Helo,' – the name given to the helicopter forces at Brindisi – the war was fairly uneventful. Hundreds of hours were spent sitting alert for the call that fortunately never came. During the campaign, SOF helicopters provided the initial response to the rapidly expanding refugee situation in nearby Albania. Thousands of pounds of emergency food rations and sleeping bags were flown to camps set up near the border. Once again the SOF crews exhibited their greatest quality, flexibility. Some criticism followed the CSAR missions, mostly because they were not executed according to the standard US Air Force CSAR model. The special operations crews planned, trained, and executed the missions using the tactics and procedures unique to SOF, not CSAR. While there were some minor problems, the helicopters and crews employed by 'Task Force Helo' were the most capable in the world and they performed superbly. When they were called upon to execute, the SOF helicopter crews got the mission done each and every time. In a bombing campaign of limited goals and successes, the rescues of *Vega 31* and *Hammer 34* stand out as gleaming highlights to the world.

CHAPTER 11
CAPTAIN COURAGE
Mike Ryan

By the nature of the missions flown, America's Special Forces pilots need to have excellent flying skills. Their amazing courage and bravery enables them to perform missions that for most people would seem impossible. Over the decades, America's helicopter pilots have been involved in numerous wars and conflicts such as Korea, Vietnam, Iran, Grenada, Panama, The Gulf States, Bosnia and more recently Kosovo.

It is difficult to single out one particular incident where a pilot has shown courage and flying skills that are way beyond the call of duty, especially as there have been so many heroic actions over the years. There is however one particular incident that occurred in Grenada, during Operation 'Urgent Fury' in 1983.

This account relates to an outstanding act of bravery performed by a USMC pilot. The incident concerned took place at the height of Operation 'Urgent Fury' on 25 October 1983. The USMC crew who were cited for Americas highest bravery awards were flying an AH-1T Cobra attack helicopter assigned to the 2nd Marine Amphibious Unit. The crew consisted of two people, the pilot, Capt Tim Howard (now LtCol) and co-pilot, WSO, Capt Jeb Seagle (deceased). They had originally been on route to Beirut, Lebanon to relieve the 24th MAU when they got diverted to Grenada to participate in Operation 'Urgent Fury'. The mission had been changed on 2 October 1983, one day before 241 US service personnel lost their lives in a terrorist bombing incident in Beirut.

The purpose of Operation 'Urgent Fury' was to invade Grenada and rescue US citizens that were in possible danger from the Marxist Peoples' Revolutionary Army, who had recently taken control of the island by force against the Grenadan peoples' wishes. The 2nd MAU were tasked with providing fire-support to the ground forces and were also given the role of riding shotgun for the transport helicopters during the initial assaults.

Operation 'Urgent Fury' commenced on 25 October with an air assault by Marines using Sea Stallion helicopters. They landed near Pearls Airport at 0520 hours and 20 minutes later Army Rangers began jumping from USAF C-130s over Point Salines Airport in the South of Grenada. Throughout the invasion the USMC Cobra gunships provided robust support to the ground forces, engaging AAA systems and Cuban forces that were threatening the advance of the Marines.

During the attack on Pearls Airport, a number of Cuban and Grenadan soldiers were putting up stiff resistance against the Marines – until the Cobras were called in to take them out, arriving and quickly neutralizing cannons that were causing problems. On a nearby hill a number of enemy soldiers had pinned down the Marines with heavy gunfire from three 12.7mm machine-guns that they had dug in on well-sited positions. With the arrival of the Cobras the enemy soon fled, and the Marines were able to consolidate their position. The Cobras flew a two ship for mutual protection and were without doubt one of the best military assets deployed during 'Urgent Fury'. After their fire-mission at Pearls airport they were tasked with providing air-support to the Marines at Grand Anse Campus.

This part of 'Urgent Fury' was of key importance to the operation as most of the American medical students were based here and the main reason for US intervention was to rescue them from the PRA. The assault commenced with USMC CH-46 Sea Knights landing Marines on the nearby beach, under the protection of Cobra gunships and A-7 Corsair strike aircraft, the mission was a success and no Marines were killed.

Later in the day the Cobras were called in to provide fire-support at Calvigny Barracks where it was believed that a large force of Cubans were based. They circled the Barracks after an air-strike had taken place and confirmed that the Cubans had fled. As the Cobras withdrew to return to base for refuelling, a tragic mid-air collision took place near the barracks involving two Black Hawk helicopters. As one of the helicopters fell to the ground it landed on four Ranger Soldiers, killing them instantly.

The Cobra crews started to feel vulnerable, they had been in the thick of the fighting all day and so far they had not been hit. They were well aware of the fact that a number of US helicopters had already been shot down over Grenada that day and clearly the Cubans 23mm cannons posed a significant threat to low flying helicopters. Capt Howard and his co-pilot Capt Seagle had just flown along the coast with their support Cobra towards the recently liberated Pearls Airport, when they received a request for assistance from a detachment of Rangers that had been ambushed at Fort Frederick which overlooked Grenada's capital St. Georges.

The Rangers had come under heavy gunfire and didn't have the fire-support available to take out the threat at ground level. Nearby, another request had been put in by a SEAL team who were securing the Governor-General's residence. The two Cobra gunships approached the St. Georges area with caution. As they flew towards Fort Frederick they spotted some of the Cuban and Grenadan soldiers on the ground and began firing at them. The Cobra, flown by Capt Howard, made four passes over the enemies positions and kept firing at them until no more ammunition was available. The support helicopter flown by Maj John 'Pat' Guigerre, and co-pilot 1st Lt Jeff Sharver, also needed more ammunition so both Cobras broke off their attacks and flew back to their base for a re-supply.

The AH-1 T Cobra attack helicopters quickly re-armed and returned to the St. Georges area to pick up where they had left off. As Capt Howard lined up his Cobra for a pass at the enemy positions, all hell broke loose. Howard's Cobra was being targeted by anti-aircraft fire from a nearby mental hospital. His Cobra took multiple hits on the airframe, with three of the shots perforating the cockpit of the helicopter, causing serious injury to him. The first shot hit him in the right arm tearing it off from just below the elbow. The second shot hit him in the right leg, seriously impairing his knee causing great pain and difficulty with controlling the helicopter. The final shot caused a piece of the Cobra to break off and embed itself in his neck. Despite his serious injuries, Capt Howard managed to wrap his left arm around the control column 'stick' and bring the helicopter in to land on a field near to Saint George's beach. Capt Howard had tried to get the co-pilot, Capt Seagle to land the helicopter, however he had been knocked unconscious from the rounds hitting the airframe. Howard recalls, "He must have hit his head when we got hit, because I tried yelling his name, but he wouldn't come to. I knew I had to do something, so I tried everything I could to land safely."

During the landing, the Cobra was seriously damaged, when the tail rotor hit the ground and separated from the tail boom.

The warning lights on the circuit board lit up "like a Christmas tree", remembers Howard. As the helicopter came to a halt, Howard managed to keep it upright, however a fire broke out. Fortunately Seagle regained consciousness and was able to assist Howard in getting out of the burning Cobra. Capt Howard recalls how Seagle rescued him, "He kept yelling at me to get out, but I don't think he knew how bad I had been hurt."

Capt Howard managed to unbuckle himself from the Cobras seat, despite being in agony from his wounds. He climbed out of the cockpit and fell to the ground. As he tried to crawl away from the burning Cobra, Seagle grabbed him by the back of his shirt and dragged him to safety. "I used my good leg to push with, while he was pulling me. He left me in a tall grassy field, next to a soccer stadium," recalls Howard. Howard remembers shouting at Seagle to get away from the crash scene. He kept yelling, "You've got to get out of here. I am going to die, but you've got a chance." Howard was more concerned for Seagle's safety than his own, he was very seriously injured and at that particular time he felt his chances of survival were slim.

Seagle realized that Howard was in a critical condition, and that his only chance of survival rested with him. Seagle informed Howard that he was going to try and link up with one of the Ranger units that were nearby in Saint Georges. He managed to put a call in to his base before the helicopter became engulfed in flames, however they were very heavily committed elsewhere so he took the decision to leave Howard, feeling that without urgent medical attention he would die. Seagle left the scene and, predicting his own death, Howard thought he would never see him again.

The other Cobra gunship that Howard had been operating with over Saint Georges had picked up the distress call and was on route to the crash scene with a USMC CH-46 Sea Knight transport helicopter. As the two helicopters approached the burning wreckage of Howard's Cobra, the remaining enemy forces in the area opened fire on them. The Cobra helicopter that was providing fire-support to the rescue team started to take hits from AAA systems nearby, Howard looked on in horror as he saw his friends in the support Cobra perish as their helicopter plunged out of control into the ocean. Both Guigerre and Sharver were killed in the crash.

Over an hour had passed since Howard's Cobra went down and already two brave pilots had died in the attempt to rescue him. It was now the turn of the CH-46 to brave the AAA. As the rescue helicopter flared for landing, the enemy opened fire with everything they had. The CH-46 hit the deck hard, the door gunners opened fire on the enemy positions in an attempt to suppress their fire, but there were too many of them. Capt Howard tried to crawl towards the rescue helicopter, but he was weak from the massive loss of blood and just couldn't make it. Meanwhile, Gunnery Sgt Kelly Neideigh, a door gunner on the CH-46, risked his life by running into live fire to drag Howard back to his helicopter. Neideigh was a Vietnam veteran, and displayed outstanding courage in what was a highly lethal killing zone. With Howard aboard, the CH-46 climbed into the air and flew to a nearby medical facility. His co-pilot Capt Seagle, never made it to safety, he was sadly found dead on a nearby beach. It transpired that Seagle was captured by enemy forces and murdered.

After the rescue, Capt Howard spent many months in a hospital, learning to live with the loss of his arm. Doctors informed him that he would never walk again, however he was to prove them wrong. His wife was of great support to him during this difficult time, and he soon recovered from his injuries and fought to remain in the Marine Corps.

The Marine Corps admired Howard's determination to remain in the Service and agreed that he should be allowed to serve on, as he had become a hero within the USMC. He was assigned to various duties following his recovery, including activating the 1st Remotely Piloted Vehicle Company, based in Twentynine Palms, California. Howard received the Silver Star, the Distinguished Flying Cross with a Combat 'V', and the Purple Heart for his actions in Grenada. He also received several awards from civilian organizations honouring his courage and dedication to duty. Howard is now a Colonel in the USMC and is the 2nd Marine Division's assistant chief of staff for intelligence. The Marine Corp are very proud of their men's actions on 25 October and rightly so – these airmen displayed bravery beyond the call of duty.

CHAPTER 12
A BRIGHT FUTURE UNFOLDS
Mike McKinney

A major change is about the take place in the SOF helicopter world. In 2003, AFSOC will begin operating a new and exciting aircraft, the Bell-Boeing CV-22 Osprey. Part helicopter and part airplane, the CV-22 will revolutionize the SOF community. The CV-22 can takeoff and land like a helicopter, yet travel at turbo-prop airplane speeds. So radical is the CV-22 that a new class of aircraft – powered-lift – has been created by the aviation industry to identify its characteristics. Technically, the aircraft is a tiltrotor, creating vertical lift by tilting its prop-rotors 90 degrees to the horizontal position. After a vertical takeoff, the propro-tors are tilted forward and the Osprey becomes a turboprop air-plane. To the SOF community, the capability that the CV-22 brings is not fully realized. As can be seen throughout this book, many SOF helicopter missions have been long and stressful. This is primarily due to the slow speed of the helicopters. Eagle Claw and Son Tay are just two examples where speed could have increased the probability of success for each mission. Speed is exactly what the CV-22 brings to the fight, diminishing the time spent in enemy territory and increasing the survivability. With a 500-mile unrefuelled range and a 250-mile per hour cruise speed, the CV-22 can strike deep and strike fast.

The CV-22 is an outgrowth of the basic MV-22 flown by the US Marine Corps. In a combined purchase, the US Special Operations Command and the US Air Force have come together to fund the development of the CV version. Some of the major changes from the MV-22 are an increased fuel capacity; a Terrain Following/ Terrain Avoidance (TF/TA) radar system; and a Suite of Integrated Radio Frequency Countermeasures (SIRFC). These systems combined with the advantages of the tiltrotor design will give the CV-22 an unmatched capability in the SOF aviation world. The major advantage of the CV-22 is the ability to strike quicker than current helicopters. A CV-22 can get in and out of denied airspace in half the time of a helicopter. No matter what the SOF mission, the CV-22 will cut down the time dramatically. Another advantage is the ability to self-deploy over greater distances than helicopters. Today, most helicopters are limited to about 1200 miles for self-deployment. Given the slow speed, this equates to nearly 12 hours of flight time. Above this figure the helicopters are usually broken apart, placed on C-5 Galaxy airlifters and flown to the destination. This is a time-consuming and expensive task. On the other hand the Osprey can self-deploy up to 2100 miles meaning that SOF vertical-lift assets can be in an area quicker and ready for action. One final advantage is the ability of the CV-22 to fly at altitudes up to 25,000 feet. While the advantages for deployment can easily be seen, this also allows the Osprey to fly above many threat systems that make helicopters vulnerable.

While the CV-22 will have a positive impact on SOF operations, there is some criticism to address. First among most negative comments is the size of the aircraft. Not as large as an MH-53M and not as small as an MH-60, the CV-22 fits somewhere in the middle. It has been compared to the H-3 in terms of cabin space. This limits the number of personnel the Osprey can carry to 18. It also puts a limit on the type of equipment capable of fitting into the space. Very few vehicles or boats in the current

SOF inventory can fit inside a CV-22. This means that the customer will either have to go without, or design a new system. Probably the most severe comments concern the safety of the Osprey. Throughout its long test program, dating back into the 1980s, there have been several high-profile accidents. The most recent of these accidents occurred on 8 May 2000, resulting in the deaths of 19 Marines. The causes of each of these accidents have been found and steps taken to reduce the risk, but the reputation of the Osprey suffered a huge blow. It remains to be seen whether the safety criticism is justified. Some risk must be accepted with such a radically new technology like the Osprey, but just what level is uncertain. The introduction of the first helicopters was also fraught with numerous accidents and failures. History has shown that early doubt in helicopters was unfounded. Finally, the CV-22 is an expensive aircraft, costing the taxpayers about $40 million per copy. The impact this has on SOF is that only 50 CV-22s will be produced, far less than could be utilized. The hope is that as production increases over the years and the costs are driven down, more Ospreys will be put into service. Another option is the development of an entirely new four-engined tiltrotor the size of a C-130 Hercules.

In less than ten years the USAF will cease to be in the SOF helicopter business and a distinctive part of air power history will come to an end. After this the only dedicated US SOF helicopter force will be found in the Army's 160th SOAR. While AFSOC will go the way of the CV-22, this technology cannot be categorized as a true helicopter. The Osprey will spend the majority of its flight time as a turboprop airplane, thereby ending the existence of helicopters. In the early 1990s there surfaced a proposal to replace the ageing Pave Low fleet with brand new three-engined MH-53E Super Sea Stallions. Although with the CV-22 already on the wish list, the plan was scrapped. Ironically, although the USAF started and matured the SOF helicopter business, that history will be quickly abandoned.

Finally, it must be noted that at the time of going to publication these details are correct; however changes are always occurring in the SOF helicopter world that may not have been detailed here.

CHAPTER 13
CSAR AND SPECIAL OPERATIONS IN THE NEW MILLENNIUM
Mike Ryan

As we enter the new Millennium, changes are taking place within the Pentagon regarding the future developments of CSAR (Combat Search and Rescue) capabilities within the US armed forces.

In America, joint doctrine calls for each service branch to be responsible for its own CSAR capability. However, in most conflict situations, the USAF handles the role on behalf of the other services – within the USAF, CSAR responsibility rests with Air Combat Command (ACC). ACC operates with just a handful of squadrons equipped with HC-130 Hercules tankers and HH 60G Pave Hawk helicopters. The prime role of ACC is rescue rather than Special Forces Operations, as many people would assume. The current equipment operated by ACC is out of date and desperately in need of replacement. The unit has an urgent need for an all-weather, deep-penetrating rescue platform, such as the Black Hawk HH-60D. This helicopter was originally planned for USAF service, however due to budget restraints this model could not be purchased. As a result ACC operates the Black Hawk HH-60G, which lacks radar and infra-red equipment, making rescue work at night and in bad weather extremely difficult. With a cruising speed of just 160mph and a range of only 400 miles, they are far from ideal for CSAR.

During rescue missions the USAF normally turns to the A-10

Thunderbolt for close air support (CAS). These aircraft perform in the SANDY role and offer good fire-support capabilities to the rescue helicopters. On the other side of the fence the grass is definitely greener for the Air Force Special Operations Command (AFSOC). They have money from Congress, in addition to modern all-weather capable helicopters. Although with their main role being unconventional warfare behind enemy lines, this is hardly surprising. AFSOC operates the MC-130 Hercules and MH-53J Enhanced Pave Low 111 helicopter. This helicopter is built upon the Vietnam era 'Super Jolly Green Giant' airframe. The MH-53J is well equipped, with radar missile jammers, night-vision goggles, chaff and flare dispensers and highly sophisticated terrain-following radar and forward-looking infra-red systems.

AFSOC is in the process of buying some fifty Bell Boeing CV-22 Osprey tilt-rotor aircraft, which will enter service between 2005 and 2012. The Osprey will give the USAF a quantum leap in mission capability, as it can fly over 2,100nm with only one in-flight refuelling. The CV-22 Osprey is a hybrid cross between an aircraft and a helicopter and will be capable of a 230kt cruising speed, with a combat radius of 500nm. It combines the vertical takeoff, hover and vertical landing qualities of a helicopter, with the long range, fuel efficiency and speed of a turboprop aircraft. It is clear to see that if America had the Osprey in 1980, during the Iranian hostage crisis, the outcome of Operation 'Eagle Claw' could have been different. The CV-22 will the give the US Armed Forces a capability that is unique only to them. As a result, they will have the ability to carry out missions that before now, would have been impossible to perform using just one type of platform.

AFSOC also operate the MC-130 Hercules and Combat

Talon aircraft in support of the Special Forces, These aircraft are equipped to perform missions at night and in bad weather. The difference between equipment used by the ACC rescue units and the AFSOC Special Operations units is enormous. This has created a difficult situation for the Pentagon, as during combat situations AFSOC is frequently called upon to carry out rescue missions, even though rescue is not part of AFSOCs responsibility. This is due to the fact that air commanders recognize that AFSOC is better equipped than dedicated ACC rescue units to carry out rescue missions, even though they hold the responsibility for the mission.

Since AFSOC pilots would like to perform the Special Operations missions that they train for, problems have arisen such as those during the recent Kosovo war; when heated arguments occurred between air commanders concerning who was going to carry out aircrew rescues – AFSOC or ACC. On one occasion in Kosovo, a pilot was almost captured because of the debates over whose job it was to carry out the rescue. This is unacceptable, as the longer a downed pilot remains on the ground, the higher the risk of him being captured. In the CSAR world, it is usually assumed that unless a pilot is rescued within four hours of being downed, he will not be rescued at all. As a result of the Kosovo war, a major review is currently taking place within the Pentagon, regarding the responsibility issues raised between ACC and AFSOC.

Looking into the future, there are many new Rescue and Special Forces equipment concepts under development. These include:

Unmanned Air Vehicle (UAV) Rescue Platforms.

These are small vehicles that resemble the Osprey tilt-rotor. They would be deployed on high-risk missions, where there are greater chances of losing manned helicopters. Once the pilot has been located, a UAV would be sent in to carry out a rescue. A down side to this concept is that it assumes the pilot is uninjured and able to climb into the cabin. In many documented cases, it is a fact that pilots are usually injured or suffering from shock and as a result they would require help from a third party.

AVPRO Exint Pod

Currently undergoing evaluation by both the British and American armed forces. The AVPRO Exint (ExtractioniInsertion) Pod is a one-man pod of some 12ft in length. Designed for the speedy insertion/extraction of Special Forces and the recovery of downed aircrew, Exint can be carried on any helicopter with a weapons pylon. The concept was originally developed for the British SAS, for carriage on the Harrier Jump-Jet. However it quickly became apparent that Exint could be carried on all US attack helicopters, including the WH-64 Apache, AH-1 Cobra, Black Hawk, and RAH-66 Comanche.

In effect, Exint converts attack helicopters into CSAR platforms, allowing them to go deep behind enemy lines for the extraction of downed pilots. Should the mission be compromised, the attack helicopter can fight back, and being small there is a greater chance of evading AAA and SAMs. When not being used in the personnel carrying role, Exint can be used for the carriage of high value equipment or pilot's personal kit, this allows attack helicopters to self-deploy without the need for support helicopters. Within each pod there is a radio, GPS and air conditioning system and a state of the art parachute system. This allows the Exint Pod to be released from either an aircraft or helicopter for Special Operations. As the Pod nears the ground or water, proximity sensors fire six airbags to absorb the landing impact, these air bags then deflate forming a floatation device. Although a standard helicopter fit would be two Exint Pods, the WH-64 Apache can carry as many as four. This means that an Apache can fly up to four Delta soldiers and their kit on one mission and with the Apaches long range this is an impressive capability.

AVPRO Titan X-Wing concept.

The AVPRO Titan X-Wing has been designed to be capable of meeting the US requirement for a new heavy-lift VTOL vehicle. As such, the design proposed has a maximum payload of 60 tons and can accommodate two LAV-25 vehicles in its payload bay. It could carry a very significant defensive/offensive armament, comprising forward and rearward cannon turrets and air-to-air missiles (AIM-9L and AIM-120). To improve the combat effectiveness of the vehicle its operational range can be extended by air refuelling (AR) while the aircraft is operating in conventional mode with the X-Wing stationary. The main roles envisioned for Titan, are that of heavy-lift and Special Forces Operations, where its VTOL capabilities could be exploited at both ends of the route. Its cruise speed should be as high as possible and should definitely exceed that of existing heavy-lift helicopters such as the Chinook and Super Stallion. This benefits the field commander by not only providing quicker placement of troops and equipment, but also allowing a greater number of sorties to be performed in a given time frame. The principal features of the design are a relatively conventional fuselage to house the payload, crew, systems, and some of the fuel. Its fuselage is more streamlined than that of existing heavy-lift helicopters, since the vehicle is designed to be capable of a cruise speed in excess of 300mph (483kmh) in airplane mode.

An innovative gas-driven X-wing rotor would provide VTOL lift in the same way as a conventional helicopter rotor, but would be driven by high-pressure air bled from the twin turbofan engines. The air would exit the blades through nozzles located at the blade's tips, causing them to rotate. The rotor could be brought to rest to allow the vehicle to fly like a conventional aircraft, with the stationary rotor blades performing the same function as the wing on a fixed-wing aircraft. With the blades stationary, no bleed air would be taken from the engines, hence all the air entering the engine would be used to provide forward thrust for flight. In order to provide large payload capability (especially when operating in VTOL mode) a high-speed cruise it is essential to keep the Titan's empty weight to a minimum. For this reason, advanced composite materials, mainly carbon/epoxy, would be used for the primary structure wherever possible. Production and maintenance procedures for composites have matured rapidly and their use as the primary structural material for a new aircraft does not present a significant technological risk. Conversely, their advantages over metals, such as low weight, high strength, improved fatigue resistance, damage tolerance and negligible corrosion, make them ideally suited to the proposed vehicle and its likely operating environment.

The leading edges of the rotors contain multi-element phased array radars with electronic beam steering. This provides the crew with 360 degree radar coverage while the X-wing is rotating. With the X-wing stationary, 360 degree coverage is still maintained because each blade can cover a 90 degree scan zone. The data obtained from the radar could be data-linked from the vehicle to AWACS or JSTARS aircraft, or direct to other friendly forces. In essence, the aircraft is capable of performing reconnaissance, SIGINT or ELINT operations while carrying out its transport mission.

While the X-wing has many advantages over the pure helicopter, especially in the heavy lift transport role, another advanced hybrid is being developed as a potential replacement for the US Marine Corps AH-1 W Super Cobra attack helicopter. The Canard Rotor Wing (CRW) is being developed at Boeing's Phantom Works in St Louis, in response to a US Defence Advanced Projects Agency (DARPA) program.

No matter what platforms the US armed forces decide to operate in the future for CSAR or Special Operations, the demand will not change for the skilful flying and courage that a pilot needs to execute a mission. From Korea through to Kosovo, the pilots of the US armed forces have proudly served their country and long may they continue to do so.

SOURCES

Mike McKinney

Bergeron, Randy G. *Air Force Special Operations Command (AFSOC) in the Gulf War.* June 2000. Headquarters, Air Force Special Operations Command/Office of the Historian, Hurlburt Field, FL. USA.

Chinnery, Philip D. *Any Time, Any Place: A History of USAF Air Commando and Special Operations Forces.* 1994. Naval Institute Press, Annapolis, MD.

Des Brisay, Thomas, D. "Fourteen Hours at Koh Tang". *Air War-Vietnam.* 1978. Arno Press, New York.

Greeley, Jim. and Leach, Karl. "The Search for EBRO33". *Night Flyer.* May 1996. US Air Force Special Operations Command, Hurlburt Field, FL.

Guilmartin Jr., John F. *A Very Short War: The Mayaguez and the Battle for Koh Tang.* 1995. Texas A&M University Press, College Station, TX.

Headquarters, Pacific Air Forces. *Assault on Koh Tang.* 1975. HQ PACAF, Hickam AFB, HI.

Kern, Tony. "Case Study: Black Knight: A Mission that couldn't afford to fail." *Flight Discipline.* 1998. McGraw Hill, New York.

Kelley, Orr. *From A Dark Sky, The Story of US Air Force Special Operations.* 1996. Presidio Press, Novato, CA.

MacKenzie, Richard. "Apache Attack" *Air Force Magazine.* Oct. 1991. Air Force Association, Arlington, VA.

McKenna, Ken and Wright, Ken. "To the Rescue", *Airman Magazine*, Feb. 2000. Air Force News Agency, Kelly AFB, TX.

McRaven, William H. *Spec Ops, Case Studies in Special Operations Warfare: Theory and Practice*. 1995. Presidio Press, Novato, CA.

Morse, Stan. *Gulf Air War Debrief*. 1991. Aerospace Publishing Ltd, London.

Schemmer, Benjamin F. *The Raid*. 1976. Harper & Row, New York.

Waller, Douglas C. *The Commandos: The Inside Story of America's Secret Soldiers*. 1994. Simon and Schuster, New York.

The majority of the information comes from the author's personal recollections of the nights in question and via briefings given by various crewmembers involved. Also, the author has discussed the missions with the crewmembers at length.

Mike Ryan

Adams, James. *Secret Armies: Inside the American, Soviet and European Special Forces*. 1987. Atlantic Monthly Press, New York.

Beckwith, Col Charles. *Delta Force*. 1983. Harcourt Brace Jovanovich, New York.

Bowden, Mark. *Black Hawk Down: A Story of Modern War*. 1999. Penguin, London.

Evans, Andy. *Combat Search and Rescue*. 1999. Arms and Armour, London.

Nadel, Joel with Wright, J.R. *Special Men and Special Missions:*

Inside American Special Operations Forces 1945 to the Present. 1994. Greenhill Books, London.

Information was also collected from various US Defence Libraries and US Historical Societies.